SOUND DESIGNS

SOUND DESIGNS

▼ ▼ ▼ ▼ ▼ ▼ ▼ ▼ ▼ ▼ ▼ ▼ ▼ ▼ ▼ ▼

A HANDBOOK OF MUSICAL
INSTRUMENT BUILDING

REINHOLD BANEK &
JON SCOVILLE

Photographs by Elizabeth McBride-Smith
Illustrations by Dick Obenchain

↑☉ **TEN SPEED PRESS**
Berkeley, California

Permission to quote from *Lou Harrison's Music Primer* has been kindly granted by the publisher, C. F. Peters Corp., 373 Park Avenue South, New York, N.Y. 10016.

1☉
TEN SPEED PRESS
P.O. Box 7123
Berkeley, CA 94707

Design by Catherine Jacobes
Photographs by Elizabeth McBride-Smith
Illustrations by Dick Obenchain

Library of Congress Cataloging-in-Publication Data
Banek, Reinhold.
    Sound designs / Reinhold Banek & Jon Scoville : photographs by Elizabeth McBride-Smith : illustrations by Dick Obenchain.
        p.   cm.
    Includes bibliographical references.
    ISBN 0-89815-775-7
    1. Musical instruments--Construction.   I. Scoville, Jon.
II. Title.
ML460.B18   1995
784.192'3--dc20   95-35931
                                                                                      CIP
                                                                                      MN

First printing this edition, 1995
Printed in Canada

    2 3 4 5 — 99 98 97 96

Distributed in Australia by E. J. Dwyer Pty. Ltd., in Canada by Publishers Group West, in New Zealand by Tandem Press, in South Africa by Real Books, and in the United Kingdom and Europe by Airlift Books.

CONTENTS

▼ ▼ ▼ ▼ ▼ ▼ ▼ ▼ ▼ ▼ ▼

METAL

▼ ▼ ▼ ▼ ▼ ▼ ▼ ▼ ▼ ▼ ▼

SKIN

▼ ▼ ▼ ▼ ▼ ▼ ▼ ▼ ▼ ▼ ▼

PLASTIC

▼ ▼ ▼ ▼ ▼ ▼ ▼ ▼ ▼ ▼ ▼ ▼

GLASS

▼ ▼ ▼ ▼ ▼ ▼ ▼ ▼ ▼ ▼ ▼

▼ ▼ ▼ ▼ ▼ ▼ ▼ ▼ ▼ ▼ ▼ ▼

APPENDIX

ACKNOWLEDGEMENTS

IN THE YEARS THAT WE HAVE BEEN WORKING on this book many people in many ways have given us time, assistance, and encouragement.

A posthumous thank-you goes to the spirit of Harry Partch, whose adventurous nature and unique experiments with instruments have been a continual source of inspiration. Lou Harrison and Bill Colvig keep that spirit alive in many ways. They are constantly investigating unlikely materials and inventing new instruments. They have been generous with ideas and advice whenever we were stuck with a problem of acoustics or design. Mel McBride helped us greatly with his suggestions and his loan of a strobe tuner. And thanks go to Gordon Mumma for the use of his frequency counter and his general enthusiasm for the unusual. And to Ron Taylor for his donation of the maple for the temple blocks.

Michael Spiro and Dennis Broughton have been wonderful teachers of percussion and Latin American instrumental technique. Michael provided much of the rhythmic information for this book. Deanna Smith and Bill Harren showed us the finger cymbal rhythm. Collin Walcott gave us advice on the amadinda. And Paul Hostetter helped us with his recommendations for several of the books in the bibliography. Emil Richards' book on his remarkable instrument collection planted many seeds.

In his care and feeding of the *Experimental Musical Instruments* quarterly, Bart Hopkin has been instrumental in helping to raise the "children of Harry Partch." He has created a network for all those people working with wood, metal, stone, plastic, glass, baling wire, and imagination to add new instruments to a lineage which goes back most recently to Leo Fender and Adolph Sax and beyond that to all the anonymous builders who helped put music on our planet. Bart has been most generous with information, time, and advice.

Thanks go to Phil Wood, George Young, and Jackie Wan of Ten Speed Press for their accommodation, good counsel, and forbearance. Also to Ira Friedlander for his sage advice on the task of writing and publishing a book. Linelle Lane and Kathy Caton were remarkable in their ability to decipher illegible manuscripts and quickly come up with clean typewritten copies.

Stephen Tortorici and Mu Tongsuk deserve gratitude for their marvelous Thai restaurant, Kninnari, which served food in many forms while the manuscript was in its final stages. Thanks to Eduardo Izquierdo for looking after our animals as well as introducing us to our illustrator. To Alan Savat for his care and attention to details that would otherwise have taken time away from this book. And to Mac Hartley who aided and abetted us in many ways with his multiple talents. A hug to Roberta Bristol for her warm heart, her home, and her hot tub, which eased tired bodies during the building process.

We have been particularly fortunate to be able to work with Betty Smith and Dick Obenchain. Betty's remarkable photographs have given each instrument a life of its own. Dick's lucid illustration, by clarifying the text, made the task of writing this book much easier.

Lastly, thanks to Tandy and all the other friends who provided support, patience, enthusiasm, and love throughout.

PREFACE TO THIS EDITION

HAVE YOU EVER FOUND YOURSELF WALKING up to a washing machine running on its spin cycle? The load is a little off kilter. Yet instead of turning off the machine to balance it, you use your hands on top of the washer to play along with the rhythm it's making? Or have you ever tapped out a rhythm on the dashboard of your car in time with the radio as you drive down the road? If so, then you have demonstrated that you have A) that incurable and highly contagious disease called "rhythmitis," and B) you have been scratching that "rhythmitis" by using "Found Sounds."

I've been a Found Sound person all my life, testing the resonances of the universe around me by hitting anything with my hands or with sticks to see what it sounds like: upside-down trash cans, aluminum lighting poles, my kid sister, etc. And as a result of my curiosity, I've collected several garages full of sound by picking up stuff at flea markets, yard sales, and trash heaps. When I took my collection of cast iron pot lids and hung them with string on a wood frame, I realized that I'd made my first instrument.

So upon discovering *Sound Designs* in 1982, I knew I'd found a gold mine of information and guidance that propelled me deeper into my journey of sound exploration and instrument building. Jon Scoville and Reinhold Banek had traveled far along this path of discovery and experimentation. And they had amassed their collective knowledge into an easy-to-follow guide. I started with some of the easy projects in this book. With the helpful hints and suggestions peppered throughout the pages, I slowly developed my woodworking and tinkering skills by doing more complex projects. After a while I was making marimbas and drums, and after a bit longer while, I found that I had become co-owner of a company that makes African-inspired instruments, and I was designing a signature series for another drum manufacturer.

Sound Designs may not necessarily send you down the same path that I've taken, but it will give you years of pleasure. Even now when I open up this book, I find new ideas and inspirations. If you are into percussion and sound, you'll soon find that it's as much fun to make the instruments as to play them. And within these pages are the seeds to help you create the instruments you may need to scratch your "rhythmitis."

Arthur Hull

*Making an instrument is one of music's greatest
joys. Indeed, to make an instrument is in some
strong sense to summon the future. It is,
as Robert Duncan has said of composing,
"A volition. To seize from the air its forms."
Almost no pleasure is to be compared
with the first tones, tests & perfections of an
instrument one has just made. Nor are all
instruments invented & over with,
so to speak. The world is rich with models
—but innumerable forms, tones & powers
await their summons from the mind & hand.
Make an instrument—you will learn
more in this way than you can imagine.*

— LOU HARRISON'S MUSIC PRIMER

INTRODUCTION

THIS IS A BOOK ABOUT MAKING THINGS that make sound. It is also about the satisfaction that comes from turning raw materials and unlikely objects into instruments capable of a wide range of sonic textures. As such, it is an exploration of the ways in which lumber, metal scraps, discarded baseball bats, toilet-tank floats, automobile parts, oxygen tanks, tired kitchen pots, sewer pipe, and other flotsam of the 20th century can become the means for making music. And it is a collaboration between a musician fascinated by all aspects of sound, and a builder who loves designing and making the tools used for that purpose.

Some years ago we decided to combine our enthusiasms. We began initially by duplicating other instruments, but soon we were inventing our own. And as we progressed we kept notes on what worked and what didn't. Gradually those notes turned into this book. In a sense, then, it is both a how-to book and a journal of our discoveries. It is also a passing-on of information gathered from observing what other instrument makers have been up to—from Africa to California and from the Stone Age to the Space Age.

HOW TO USE THIS BOOK: The instruments are organized loosely into groups according to the materials from which they are made—wood, metal, skin, plastic, and glass. Along the way we have inserted chapters on scales, resonators, and instrument stands. These appear at those points where the information becomes necessary for succeeding chapters. In the appendix the instruments are divided into relative degrees of building difficulty. This will enable you to jump into the book wherever you think your tools, talent, and interests converge.

In describing how-to-do-it we suggest the method we found to be fastest and/or easiest. But since this often involves power tools, we give, wherever feasible, alternative ways which use more common hand tools.

Many of the instruments require no previous building experience—and none of them require any proficiency in music. By constructing some of the simpler instruments, you will pick up building skills which will enable you to move on to more complex designs—and in the process your musical talents may develop as well.

WHO CAN USE THIS BOOK: Parents, teachers, woodworkers, musicians, craftspeople, modern dancers, old friends with time to share, old enemies who want to beat their weapons into bells and their plow discs into gongs, people who hate music but love to build things, people who love music but have never tried playing an instrument, theatres in need of sound effects, composers in need of new resources, feminists, masculinists, Buddhists, Presbyterians, popes, and mullahs, oil executives with empty 55-gallon drums, common folk tired of petroleum politics with lots of cars and no place to go. Among others.

In essence it is a book for everyone. But it is not complete. We've left out plans for such instruments as violins, guitars, and flutes. There are already good books available on these and we have listed several in the bibliography. We also don't consider our plans to be in any way final. In fact, we would be delighted if you find easier and better ways to make them. In the process of perfecting these instruments you may soon start inventing your own and exploring garages, basements, flea markets, and junkyards in search of new designs for sound.

That was the introduction to this book written fifteen years ago. Now, as we slouch towards the millennium, we seem to have more of everything. More people are on this fragile, lovely planet. More televisions tuned to our peculiar rituals of menace and money. More garage sales to get rid of more things, more scrap metal, more scrap battleships, more scrap scrap—and more people discovering that music hath charms. Thus more garage bands playing whatever suits their fancy (if not the neighbors'). One guy even told us that he thought *Sound Designs* was cool because he was a "noise-ician" in a band, and he had found lots of ideas within these pages of ways to make noise. So whatever your reason to join in the great planetary orchestra, that even now is tuning up all over the globe, you can find something here with which to make a song. And if you put your ear close to the earth, you may be able to hear the faint golden sounds of the gongs in a gamelan in a village in Bali, the jovial wheeze of a Cajun accordion in Louisiana, the click of claves starting up a rumba in Havana, the cuica's screech and moan singing a samba in the streets of Rio, the thwock of a temple block in a quiet zendo in Kyoto, the joyous chirp of kalimbas in Burundi, and amadindas in Rwanda. Trust your ears and listen.

BASIC WOODWORKING

BEFORE WE BEGIN, HERE'S A DISCLAIMER: There is no way that a short chapter in a book on musical instruments can adequately explain the mysteries of woodworking, or the mysteries of anything else for that matter. In fact, even long chapters in a large book on woodworking will never replace the experience to be derived from actually making things yourself, or working with someone who has a real understanding of shop techniques and can guide you through the difficult spots. That said, here's a short chapter on the mysteries of woodworking in a book on musical instruments.

First, select the right tool and the right material for the job. If you must buy tools, you will be better off buying quality. Second, plan ahead—draw diagrams. If any of the explanations or illustrations in this book seem unclear (heaven forbid), then draw up your own version *before* you start cutting. This will save you time and material, both precious commodities these days. Third, take accurate measurements—twice-checked if you are not used to measuring. Fourth, if you are confronted with a new building technique, practice first.

Here is a basic list of tools needed:

HAMMERS

You will need a carpenter's hammer with a smooth face and a medium weight, around 16 ounces. Too light and you will have to work too hard to drive your nails, too heavy and you'll end up with the carpenter's version of tennis elbow. If you've never used a hammer much, practice first. Most of the power of the stroke comes from the wrist. Make sure when you start a nail that you hold it near the top. That way if you hit your fingers, they will not be crushed against whatever it is you are nailing into. Try not to nail too close to the end of a board or you will split the wood. If you must nail near the end, drill a pilot hole or cut off the tip of the nail first with some nail cutters or heavy duty wire cutters. This permits the nail to crush the fibers of the wood rather than wedging them apart.

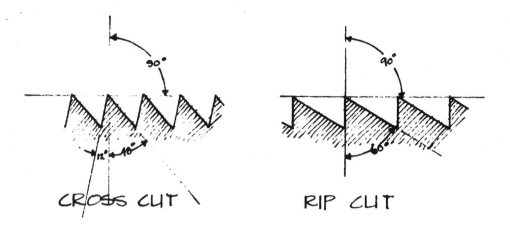

CROSS CUT   RIP CUT

SAWS

Most commonly used will be a cross-cut saw and a ripsaw. The cross-cut is designed to cut across a board against the grain. Both edges of the teeth angle away from a line perpendicular to the teeth. A ripsaw cuts with the grain down the length of a board. Its teeth have one edge that is perpendicular and one edge at an angle. When using a saw, it is best to exert pressure on the downstroke.

A relatively inexpensive power tool is the sabre saw. It will speed up your cutting and can rip, cross-cut, or cut circles. The main drawback of a sabre saw is that the blade may bend or not be positioned properly and the resulting cut will suffer. But it is faster than a handsaw and cheaper than a radial arm or table saw.

However, if you can afford to invest in one large power tool, the radial arm saw may be the most useful. It does just about anything a table saw will do, plus a few things it won't, and it's fast, accurate, and relatively safe.

DRILLS

A handbrace will equip you to do some of the drilling in this book. But for any extensive work, a power drill may be your single best cheap electric tool. For a relatively small investment it will save you time, effort and blisters. The ones with variable speeds are the most versatile. *Consumer Reports* is a good source of advice on price and dependability.

PLANES

The handiest plane for the instruments in this book is a small, low-angle, block plane made by Stanley. Planes are good devices for equaling out any small measuring or cutting errors.

CHISELS

Chisels are wood-removing tools like planes, but they are designed to cut deeper and to work in more specific places. If you can afford two chisels, get $1/2$ and 1-inch sizes, but otherwise a $3/4$-inch chisel will be an adequate compromise. If you use the chisel with the bevel facing up, you will go faster but with less control—one of life's typical trade-offs.

NAILS

The most common size nail for the projects in this book will be 4d finishing nails. The "d" stands for penny, which is what they used to cost per hundred. You can also use box nails. With their wide head, they are easier to drive but don't look as nice. A nail set will allow you to sink your finishing nails slightly beneath the surface of the wood for a better appearance. The resulting holes can be filled with putty.

SCREWS

When we suggest using screws, you should generally use #8 sheet rock screws. To facilitate this process, it is best to drill a slightly smaller pilot hole for your screw and also to use a screwdriver with a long shaft and a large handle for more twisting power.

GLUES

White glues such as Weldwood waterproof glue are dependable and do not set up so fast that they force you to rush. However, if you are in a hurry, try a 5-minute epoxy.

ABRASIVES AND SANDERS

A good versatile sanding device is 120 Grit 3M garnet paper on a rubber sanding block. This is useful for smoothing out rough edges on most wooden surfaces and for sanding down between coats of paint. If you can afford it, an orbital sander such as the Rockwell Speed Block does a spiffy job and is quick, too.

CLAMPS

A pair of 6-inch C-clamps are good to have for many of the gluing jobs. They can also be used as a vise to hold objects securely to your work table when you are cutting or drilling. Since they create a pressure of nearly six tons, they are definitely a serious tool. Pipe clamps are more expensive items but you can rent a pair if you are going to glue large surface tops for instruments like the marimbula.

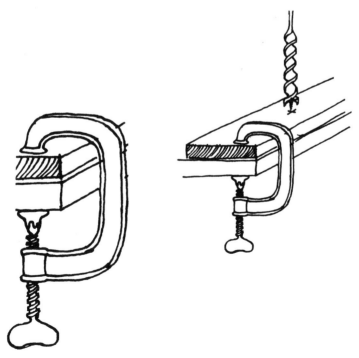

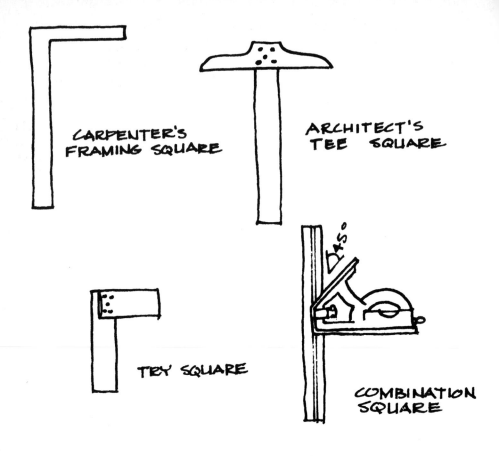

CARPENTER'S FRAMING SQUARE

ARCHITECT'S TEE SQUARE

TRY SQUARE

COMBINATION SQUARE

SQUARES

A must for any kind of accuracy in measuring, a combination square can be used for several purposes. A framing square, while less versatile, allows you to draw straight lines over longer distances.

WOOD

When you go to the lumberyard for wood for the tops to your instruments, you should look for clear heart, vertical grain, quarter-sawn wood. This is the best cut for the most efficient transmission of sound waves. And the best wood in that category is spruce, used for centuries in fine guitars and violins. Spruce is becoming harder to obtain, so redwood or cedar make good substitutes.

Clear heart means that the
board has no knots or sap wood.
Vertical grain indicates that the
line of grain is parallel to the
edge of the board. Quarter-sawn is a
method of sawing where the boards are
cut along the radial lines of the log.

Make sure that you pick out your own pieces,
and don't hesitate to go through a lot of wood in
search of just the one you want. Get into the habit of holding a prospective board at the node—about a quarter of the
length from the end—and hitting with your fist or knuckle to hear
how clear the tone is. Also, listen for duration and sweetness.
Check the end for a fine, tight, even grain. The dryer the wood, the
better it will sound. Most wood nowadays is dried in a kiln, but
sometimes you can obtain air-dried wood. This is generally better
quality than kiln-dried. However, there may still be some moisture
left in the wood. So if you are going to use it, first rough cut it to
the general size you need and then, if you're not in any hurry, let the
piece sit around in your shop for at least a year to stabilize. Kiln
dried wood can be used right away.

And remember Reinhold's Thirty-seventh Law: the better the
quality of your wood, the better the instrument will sound.

Plywoods are cheaper than most regular woods, and stronger,
too, but they are not as musical or as beautiful. So when you are
economizing, use the best wood you can afford for your tops and
sounding boards, and use plywood for all the rest. A little paint in
the right places will hide any surface defects.

Final instructions. If you start to get serious about woodworking, check out the adult education classes offered in most communities. Also, the bibliography in the back of this book suggests
woodworking books that go into tools and shop techniques in
greater detail.

Proceed with caution around all power tools and hand tools as
most are capable of biting you. Be aware of their capabilities and
limits. Learn to love and care for your tools and materials, and you
will end up loving the process of using them to make instruments.
And the care will be evident in the final results.

FELT-TIPPED MALLETS

BALL BAT BONGERS

MALLETS, BEATERS, & BONGERS

Most of the instruments in this book are members of the percussion family—they need to be struck to sound. So we will start with several easy ways to make mallets. It is important to have an assortment of varying weights and hardnesses. Often, the sound quality of an instrument will depend on what is used to strike it. With bells and gongs, a mallet that is too light or too hard will only bring out the higher overtones in the metal, and the resulting sound will be thin. If the mallet is too soft, the tone will be muffled, and of short duration. Or you may break an instrument with too heavy a mallet. Superball beat beaters sound excellent on most wooden drums but too brazen on most skin drums. So make the mallets in this book and be on the lookout for conventional drum beaters at the flea market. The more you have, the better equipped you will be to test out potential materials for instruments, and to get the best possible sound from any instrument you have made.

FELT-TIPPED MALLETS

Good tympani mallets are an expensive item, $20-$30 at music stores, and the felts wear out quickly. Here's a cheap and easy way of making your own. They will work on tympani, tube drums, and many other kinds of skin drums. What you will need is $1/2$ yard of heavy-duty felt, a 3-foot long length of $7/16$-inch dowel, two $1 1/4$-inch diameter ball knobs available in the drawer handle section of a hardware store, and a small roll of 16 gauge wire—steel, copper, or aluminum. We found the felt at a tent and awning shop, though it can often be obtained or ordered as insulation at hardware stores. Ours was a thick felt used for lining horse blankets, and while not particularly handsome, it is quite durable.

To begin, take your dowel and cut two 14-inch lengths. Next, enlarge the hole in your ball knobs with a $7/16$-inch drill bit. Make sure that you don't drill all the way through—$3/4$ to 1 inch deep is sufficient. Add a little glue to the dowel end and insert into the ball knob.

While this is drying, cut out two pairs of felt circles with diameters of approximately 6$\frac{1}{2}$ and 5$\frac{1}{2}$ inches. We used the tops of various sized jars to draw our circles. Next, cut two pieces of soft wire about 7 inches long. Lay your felt circles on top of each other, the larger one on the outside, then wrap them around the ball knob. Now take your wire, and with some pliers pull it as tightly as possible around the felt and twist. Don't twist too much or the wire will break. If you don't like the loose ends of the felt, wrap them with tape or cut them off. For a final touch you can put a slight bevel on the end of the handle and paint it.

BALL BAT BONGERS

This is an ideal mallet for the bigger oxygen tank bells and for plowdisc gongs. Garage sales and flea markets are a good place to find tired baseball bats. Only the handle half need be in good condition, so you should be able to buy them for $2 or less. And worn out baseballs and softballs should cost about $1.

Cut the handle end to a length of about 16 inches. If you have access to a lathe, attach the length to it and with a skew chisel shape the bat handle to your liking and turnout the end so that it has a hollow into which the ball can nestle. If you don't have a lathe, it will be sufficient just to bolt the ball securely to the end of the bat. Next, drill a $\frac{5}{16}$-inch hole through the center of the ball. Take a $\frac{5}{16}$-inch lag bolt which is 2 inches longer than the diameter of your ball. Slot the threats with a hacksaw or file. This insures that the bat won't split when the ball is bolted on. Now, drill out a pilot hole with a $\frac{1}{4}$-inch bit and attach the ball to the bat with your slotted lag bolt.

SUPERBALL BEATERS

SUPERBALL BEATERS

The discovery of the high bounceability of compressed silicon has been a boon to percussionists. Superballs have the ability to draw tone out of wood and plastics in a way in which no other mallet can, and it is the existence of these bouncy beaters which really makes possible the development of the slit drums, the square boos, and the bosalabos.

The best place to find superballs is in toy stores, or the toy departments of large drug or variety stores. We keep buying them in large supply for fear that the manufacturers will treat them like a fad and at some point withdraw them from the market. Superballs also tend to disappear for no apparent reason. Drop one accidentally and you'll see why. You should purchase them in various diameters so that you can have a good selection for different size wood drums. We use dowels or chopsticks for handles.

The main trick to assembling the mallets is to get the stick into the ball without it splitting in all directions. Because superballs are made from such highly compressed material, they are unstable and do not take kindly to having a foreign object inserted into them. So drill a hole first. For the small balls use a hand or electric drill with a bit that is the same size or slightly smaller than the handle of the mallet. Drill halfway through the ball trying to be as precise as possible in centering the hole. Taper the handle a bit with a knife or file before inserting it slowly into the ball, twisting as you push. Put a tad of epoxy in the hole when you put in the stick, and the little guy will never run away from home.

On the larger balls, the hole should be slightly larger than your handle for the first $1/4$ inch of the way, and then the bit should be changed to one the same size or slightly smaller than your handle. Clamp the ball in a vise as you drill and be sure not to turn the vise too tightly or you will distort the shape of the ball and make an uneven hole.

WOOD

SLIT DRUMS

SLIT DRUMS

Simple, wonderfully bubbly-sounding instruments, the slit drums are derivations of African log drums. Other versions are the tepo-naztli found in Central America and the mu yu in China. To build one is Functional Carpentry Lesson #1. Simply make an enclosed, rectangular box and cut slits into the top so as to form two "tongues." Sounds easy. However, the first box that Jon made was disastrous—wrong measurements, out of square, ill-fitting, and ugly. The amazing thing was—it sounded great. So, for those of you who are woodworking novices, here are a couple of suggestions on basic box-making which should help minimize the disasters.

Know that standard wood sizes are not what they appear to be. There hasn't been an honest 2x4 in years. Same with 1x2, 1x3, 2x2, and all the rest. For instance, a 1x6 is actually somewhere between $5/8$ and $3/4$ inches by $5^1/2$ inches. So take these discrepancies into consideration when measuring, cutting, or drawing up plans.

The easiest way to join wood at the edges is with a butt joint. It's quick, not very elegant, but strong enough for the designs in this book. Be sure to glue both edges for a better bond.

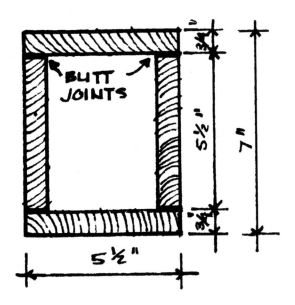

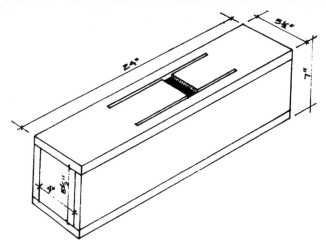

Now, for starters let's make a two-foot-long drum out of 1x6s. You can make a slit drum generally any length, although the longer it is the deeper the box should be. Cut four pieces of wood 2 feet long, and two pieces for your ends 4 by 5^1/$_2$ inches. The sides and bottom can be any cheap wood (plywood, pine, etc.). The top should be the best piece you can find and afford. Redwood has a nice warm tone. Douglas fir has bite. Spruce is the best but costly. And cedar projects well.

After cutting out the six pieces necessary, start your nails on the four sides. If looks aren't a consideration, box nails work well. Otherwise, use finishing nails. Put the first nails in about ^{3}/$_4$ inches from the edge and space them 2 inches apart. Use Elmer's, or any good wood glue, on all the edges. Then, with the aid of a vise, nail two boards together. Repeat the same process with the next board. Before you nail on the last side, nail in your end pieces. If the fit is not level, use a surform rasp or plane before fitting the top. Always glue both edges for a better bond.

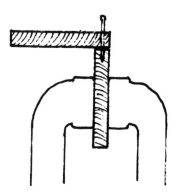

Once the top is on, mark out the lines for your tongues: $4\frac{1}{2}$ by 3 inches and $5\frac{3}{4}$ by 3 inches with an inch for the space in between the tongues will produce an interval of approximately a third, depending on the wood used. We found that ratios of one tongue length to the other of 3 to 4, 2 to 3, and 4 to 5 give pleasing intervals between the two tones. Make sure your tongues aren't cut too long and therefore structurally weak, or too short and unable to take full advantage of the tone possibilities of the box. The combined length of the two tongues plus the hole should be around 40% of the total length of the box.

After marking out the tongues and the center hole, drill a hole in the middle large enough to allow a sabre or keyhole saw to get in and cut out the center and the slits. Sand off the rough edges, take a set of superball mallets and play. If you don't like the tone, try lengthening one tongue a bit by cutting the slits a little longer. Not too much at a time, though, because you can end up cutting it too long and have the tongue split on the first strong blow. Some versions of slit drums that we've seen have a $\frac{1}{4}$-inch hole drilled at the end of each slit to help prevent splitting.

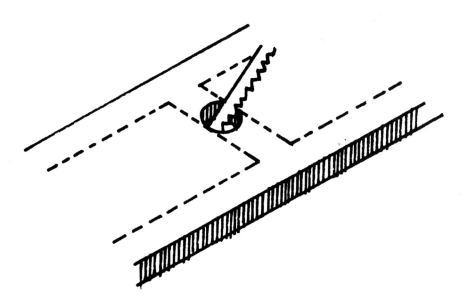

SQUARE BOOS

We were fooling around with possible variations on the slit drum when we came upon this design: an open-ended box with a tongue at one end. Ideally, each box will have the same resonant frequency as its tongue. But if you don't have an oscilloscope for precise timing, you can still produce an instrument of remarkable richness by using the following example.

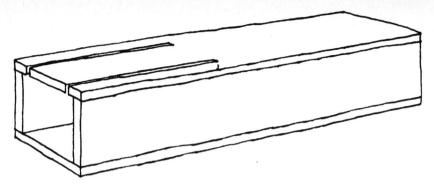

The boxes are made with sides and bottoms of $^5/_8$-inch plywood, the tops are $^3/_4$-inch quarter-sawn vertical grain redwood. Here are the dimensions. Our biggest and littlest boxes are about the outside limits for this thickness of redwood top. If you want more notes you might want to make your scale hexatonic, or even chromatic. Ours is a pentatonic version with a range of $3^1/_2$ octaves.

Width of Box	Length of Box	Length of Tongue	Width of Box	Length of Box	Length of Tongue
7″	24″	14 ¼″	5$^1/_2$″	16″	6$^1/_2$″
7″	22″	13″	5$^1/_2$″	14$^1/_2$″	6″
6″	23$^3/_4$″	11$^3/_4$″	5$^1/_2$″	14″	5$^1/_2$″
6″	22″	10$^1/_2$″	4″	14″	6″
6″	20″	10″	4″	13″	5 $^1/_2$″
6″	18″	8$^1/_2$″	4″	12″	5″
6″	17″	8″	4″	11″	4$^3/_4$″
5$^1/_2$″	20″	8$^3/_4$″	4″	10″	4″
5$^1/_2$″	18″	8″			

We tuned the instrument by ear. More precise tuning can be done by direct comparison with a pitch pipe, piano, or by using an electronic tuning device. Fine tuning is achieved by cutting the tongue longer to lower the pitch or sanding the tongue shorter—most easily done with an electric belt sander—to raise the pitch. Or if there has been a gross miscalculation, then you can cut off the entire end of the box with a skilsaw or table saw, or more laboriously with a hand saw. Note that if your tongue becomes longer than half the length of the box you weaken it structurally and are in danger of having it crack when played hard.

Now the next step, and it is the difficult part of building this instrument, is to construct a stand. We tried two different approaches at first, both of which you should avoid. We had some heavy-duty metal, left over from a pick-up truck lumber rack. So we thought, ha!, we can turn this into a handsome, sturdy stand to hold our square boos—called square boos after their similarity in design to Harry Partch's boos which were made from bamboo and were round. So after much welding, filing, painting, and general sweat work, the boxes were bolted into place. When they were played, to our dismay they gave out a most dismal "clunk" with no tone whatsoever. What we soon realized was that the stand's big feature—that it held everything securely—was also its big sonic drawback. The instrument was secure to the point of rigidity, and the resonating boxes, unable to move, no longer resonated. So we decided to try something a little less secure—precariousness being a fact of life and perhaps a part of music. We came up with a suspension system whereby the boxes had holes drilled in the sides, cord run through the holes, and then were hung between eyebolts. But this turned out to be too shaky and the boxes clanked against the eyebolts when played.

So our third attempt, and the one that finally proved to be satisfactory, was to build a two-tiered stand with the following shape and dimensions: We drilled two $3/8$-inch holes in the bottom of each box (see next page), about 8 inches apart for the bottom row, and 5 inches apart for the top row. The holes were set in $1/2$ of the distance from the end. Then we placed two bolts beneath where each of the boxes' holes would be. The bolts were $2^{1}/_{2}$ inches long and $1/4$ inch in diameter. After they were bolted in place, we cut the heads off and slipped a rubber sleeve over each bolt shaft. Next we glued two strips of polyurethane foam along the rows of bolts. You may want to use different thicknesses of foam so that the boxes' top surfaces are all on the same level.

The boxes were then mounted on the bolts, the final tuning done, and the instrument was ready to play. We found that the best sounds are produced with superball beaters of different sizes, depending on what register you are playing in. Spare boxes with different notes can be constructed and used to change the scale of your instrument at any time.

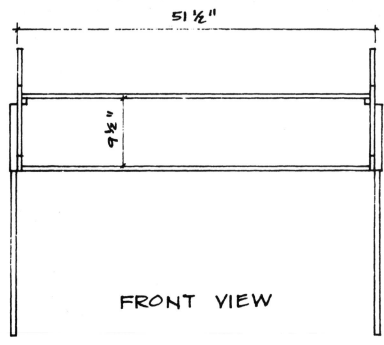

FRONT VIEW

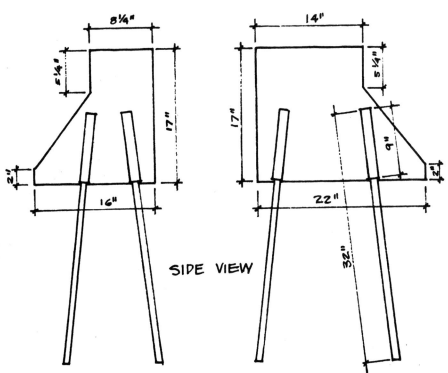

SIDE VIEW

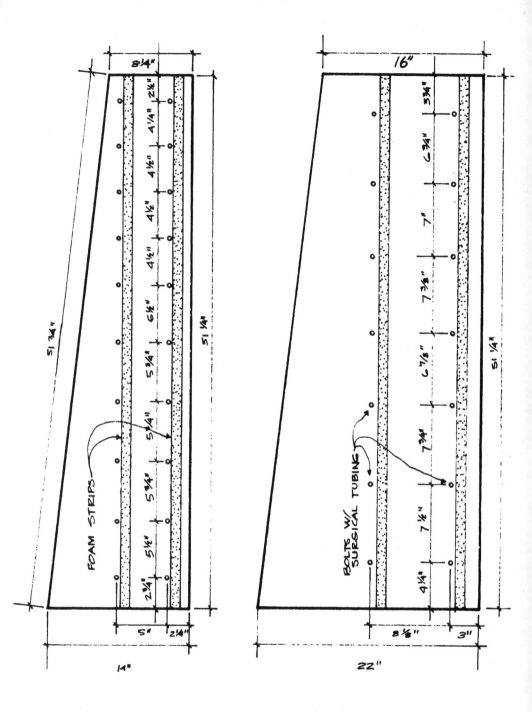

TOP LEVEL   BOTTOM LEVEL

23

WOOD BLOCKS

24

WOOD BLOCKS

Here's one of the most basic of all instruments to make and play. The wood block in its many versions can be found in almost every culture. It is simply a section of hardwood with two slits cut into it on opposite sides at opposite edges.

A piece of walnut, 3 by 3 inches and 8 to 10 inches long, is the only material you need. Trouble is, the price of the wood may seem steep for so simple an instrument. In that case mahogany or any other good hard wood can be used instead. If you live near the ocean, go down to the beach after a storm. Occasionally pieces of mahogany will have washed up. Or try that proverbial source of all inexpensive material—the local flea market.

Now to make the instrument. A radial arm saw with a dado blade is the tool of choice. If you are fortunate enough to own this versatile tool, you probably know your way around wood and won't need these instructions very much.

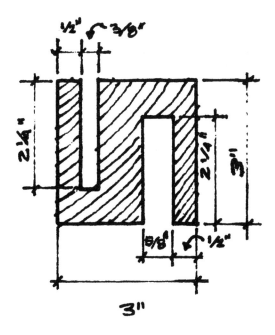

Mark off a $3/8$-inch wide slot, $1/2$ inch in from one edge of the block; $1/2$ inch in from the diametrical edge, mark off a $5/8$-inch slot. The slots should be $6^1/2$ to 7 inches long, depending on the length of your block. If you use a radial saw, put a dado blade on it or your smallest diameter blade—one with the hardest, sharpest tips you can obtain. Walnut and the other hardwoods have a habit of devouring any blade that's at all tired or not sharp enough. Center the wood beneath the saw, bracing it with a second piece of wood and a C-clamp as shown. Lock the saw into rip position. Mark $2^1/4$ inches on the lowering stem, start it up, and lower the blade into the work piece. Move carefully, but don't go too slowly or you'll have smoke. If you don't use a dado blade you will need to move your block a hair and repeat the process until the slot is the right width. Then turn the block over and use the same procedure for the other slot.

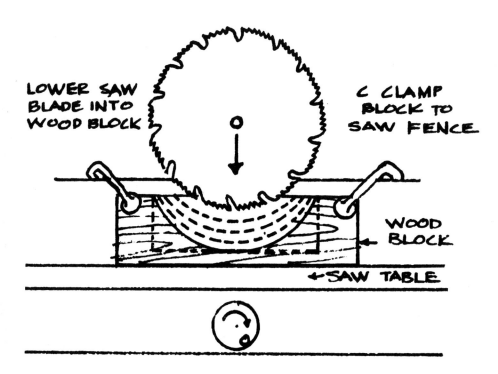

LOWER SAW BLADE INTO WOOD BLOCK

C CLAMP BLOCK TO SAW FENCE

WOOD BLOCK

←SAW TABLE

If you can't beg or borrow or rent a circular saw, or if you've given up electricity for psychological, ecological, financial, or spiritual reasons, you might want to try chiseling out the slot. This means having a good, sharp mortising chisel to use, plus callused hands and lots of endurance.

Once you've finished the sawing, you slots will look like this:

Take a chisel and remove the extra wood indicated by the dotted line. This will give you a more resonant tone. A good knocker for the block is a 6 to 8 inch piece of $3/4$-inch dowel. The addition of a little linseed oil to the outside of the instrument will bring out the warmth and color of the wood.

TEMPLE BLOCKS

Temple blocks are a high-pitched type of slit drum. They derive their name from their use in Buddhist temple ceremonies in China and Japan.

They have a bright sound like the wood block, but because they have been hollowed out their tone is more resonant. And since they are usually made in a set and tuned to a scale, they are nice to use in percussion ensembles.

We were fortunate to have been given some hard maple 1x4s that had formerly been part of a table top. Maple is an excellent wood for this venture. Other hard woods will also work but may not be as easy to obtain. You might try using a softer wood, but expect a much more muted tone.

The wood we used was a full inch thick—a rarity in the lumber industry these days. So make adjustments in your own measurements according to the wood size you use. As we suggested in the introduction to this book, the dimensions we give are only meant as general guidelines for you to work out your own proportions and choices.

TEMPLE BLOCK

The following chart gives the sizes for five temple blocks. Each block consists of six pieces of wood laminated together. Four of the pieces are a full inch thick, with the middle two having a 1-inch nipple. A fifth piece is ripped in half for the two end sections.

TEMPLE BLOCK	END PIECE SLOTS	
3 3/8″ diameter	2 1/8″ length	1/2″ width
3 1/8″ diameter	1 3/4″ length	1/2″ width
3″ diameter	1 5/8″ length	1/2″ width
2 3/4″ diameter	1 5/8″ length	1/2″ width
2 1/2″ diameter	1 1/2″ length	1/2″ width

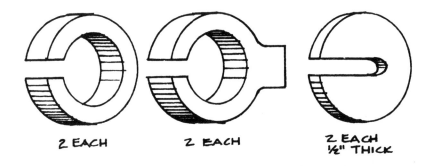

2 EACH   2 EACH   2 EACH
                                1/2″ THICK

You should rip the wood in half for the end pieces first while the stock is still square and easier to handle. Next, cut the circles out on a bandsaw. Don't forget to leave the nipples on two of each set. If you don't have access to a bandsaw, a sabre saw or a coping saw will do the job—but with somewhat more effort and less accuracy.

For glue, choose a plastic resin such as Weldwood or Wilhold. After applying the glue, hold the blocks in place with C-clamps, placing pieces of scrapwood between the clamps and the temple blocks to protect the wood. They should dry overnight, and then you can take off the glue drools and rough edges by filing and sanding. If you are in a hurry, use 5-minute epoxy.

Now for a stand. You can bolt them onto a universal stand like the one used for the red devils described on page 159. We made our stand out of a hand garden plow wheel by removing the rim and bending the spokes so they would be like long fingers to which we bolted the blocks. The two remaining spokes serve to hold a pair of agogo bells for visual and sonic contrast.

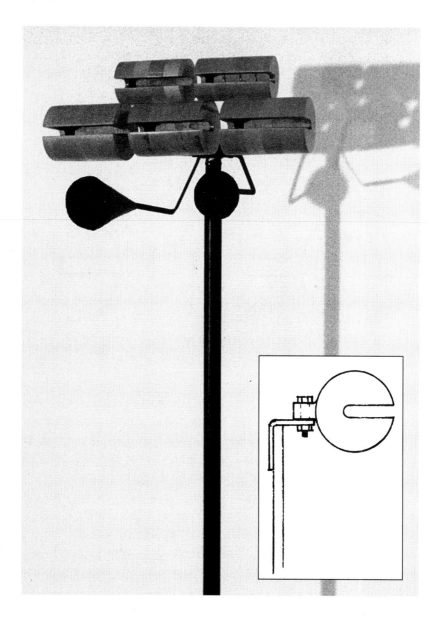

CARVED TEMPLE BLOCKS

If you enjoy carving, here's a more traditional style temple block than the laminated version given in the preceding section. You will need a block of wood at least 4 by 4 by 6 inches. You can use walnut, mahogany, or fruitwoods like pear or apple. It should be a wood that is hard enough so that it will give the nice bright tone characteristic of temple blocks, but not so hard as to dull your drills and your enthusiasm. The direction of the wood grain must run through the block from side to side with the outside of the tree being the outside or playing side of the temple block, and the inside of your tree being your handle. If you choose to carve it out of

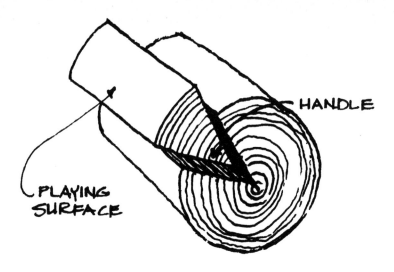

HANDLE

PLAYING
SURFACE

wood that you have cut yourself, make sure that the wood is thoroughly dry and free from splits and checks. This will spare you the dismay of having your block suddenly split down the middle.

First, rough shape the outside with a hatchet, drawknife, bandsaw, circular grinder, or whatever you have. You can form it to any of a variety of shapes but for our purposes we will describe a cylindrical version with a handle. Next, drill a 3/4-inch hole in toward the middle from each end. Locate the hole by finding the center of

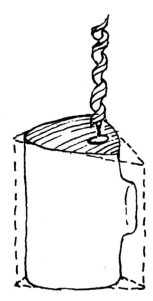

your cylinder ends and then drill the hole offset toward the handle with the edge of the hole hitting the center mark. Now saw the slot in from the outside opposite the handle toward the outside edges of the hole. There will be two saw cuts starting $^1/_2$ inch apart and ending up $^3/_4$ inches apart.

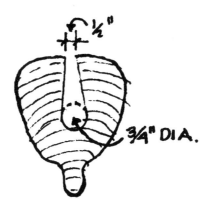

You're ready to gouge out the inside. The more wood you take out, the more you lower the pitch. It's best to leave it thicker in front and thinner toward the handle, which will give you an appropriately shaped resonant chamber. You can remove the inside wood with a hammer and gouge, or drill it out with either a brace and bit or an electric drill with a non-fluted wood bit. Or use a Foerstner bit—it's a bit which centers from its outside edge rather than from a spur in the middle, and is an excellent tool for this kind of work.

Keep removing wood from the inside of your cylinder, checking the results as you go until you hear the sound you want—a nice dry resonant THOCK. Then carve the outside to your liking. A pocket knife with a good sharp edge will do the trick. We used a small gouge and created a fluted texture on the surface. If you get really inspired, you might try carving fire-breathing dragons and painting the finished piece in traditional red and gold colors.

BOO BATS

34

BOO BATS

Remember all those baseball bats you picked up at the flea market for bongers? The ends may still be lying in the corner of your shop, their handles cut off. Well, here's how you can recycle the remaining pieces. They are nicely shaped pieces of ash, and when hollowed out will make beautiful wood blocks in the style known as Chinese piccolo blocks.

What you must do is to drill out the center of the bat. Drilling the end grain of wood is hard work and drilling hardwood end grain can be a real challenge. If you plan to use an electric hand drill for the job, you will need lots of energy and a $1/2$-inch heavy-duty drill with a very sharp bit. A muscular friend to spell you from time to time would also be useful. However, if you have access to a lathe, the project will be considerably easier.

The Milwaukee Company makes an excellent spur bit, but it's expensive. As an alternative, try a double or single spur augur bit, the kind you use with a brace, and cut off the square end so it will fit into the lathe chuck. Use a $1^{1}/_{4}$-inch diameter bit.

Attach the bat to the head stock and your bit to the tail stock chuck. The idea is to crank the handle on the tail stock, moving the stationary bit into the bat as it turns. The moment you start the lathe, you must begin feeding the bit. Move it fast enough so that the chips help cool the bit. If you start getting smoke, you are going too slowly and/or you have a dull tool. If you've never drilled on a lathe before, you might want to practice first on a piece of scrap wood.

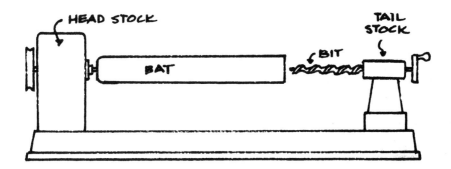

A drill press can also be used, but you will have to devise a way of holding the bat in a straight line with the bit. A vise on your drill table is a must for this operation.

Here are the dimensions for our set and the notes produced:

NOTE	DEPTH OF CUT	LENGTH OF SIDE CUT
B	$6^1/4''$	$5^3/4''$
C	$6^1/4''$	$5^3/4''$
D	$6''$	$5''$
E	$6''$	$5''$
F	$5^1/2''$	$4^3/8''$
A	$5^3/8''$	$4''$
C	$4''$	$3^1/8''$

These measurements should be considered for your purposes as only approximate. The density differences in all woods will greatly affect the pitch. Tuning is done by lengthening the slit to lower the pitch, and cutting or filing off the end to raise it.

Before you cut the side slits, you can make your Boo Bats parallel by turning them on the lathe. Fashion a cone holder that looks like this:

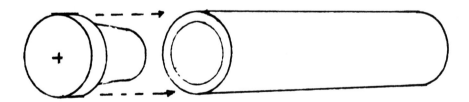

Insert it into the open end of the bat to hold it in place. Then, with a wide skew chisel, turn the bat down so that it is parallel and its walls are about ¼-inch thick. Use a large surform rasp on the bat while it turns for finishing. At this point you may want to add a decorative touch by shaping the base, and then sanding the whole piece while it is still spinning.

Remove the bat from the lathe and, at a slower speed, sand off any rough edges that remain. Drill holes into the bases and mount on a stand as shown below:

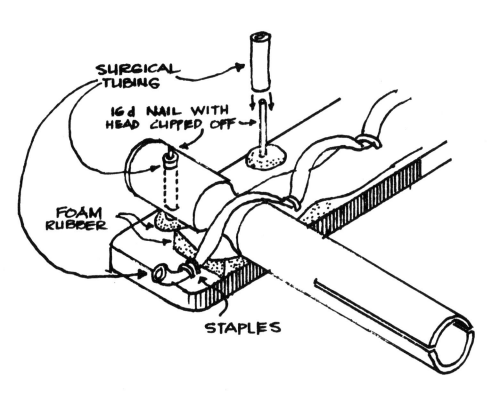

SURGICAL TUBING

16 d NAIL WITH HEAD CLIPPED OFF →

FOAM RUBBER

STAPLES

AMADINDAS

Some of the most beautiful sound in the world is to be found in the xylophone music of Africa. In it is combined melodic innocence and rhythmic sophistication to a spell-binding degree. There are types of unresonated xylophones called amadindas which are easy to build, easy to maintain, and capable of being played by two people simultaneously. Here's a simple way to construct one:

Find a 10-foot piece of dry clear heart, vertical grain, quarter-sawn redwood 2x4. Saw it to these lengths: $26^{1}/_{4}$ inches, $24^{3}/_{4}$ inches, $22^{1}/_{2}$ inches, $21^{1}/_{4}$ inches, and $20^{1}/_{4}$ inches. This will produce a pentatonic scale of sorts. But you will most likely have to do some fine tuning. To raise the pitch saw or file off wood from one of the ends. To lower it, shave or plane off from the underside center as much as is necessary to bring the tone down to where you want it. Proceed with due caution, since removal of a surprisingly small amount of wood may change the pitch more than you expect.

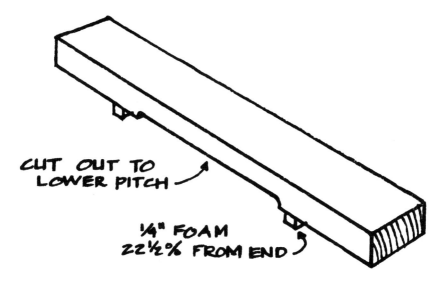

CUT OUT TO
LOWER PITCH

¼" FOAM
22½% FROM END

If redwood is unavailable, the instrument can be made out of any hard or soft wood in any dimensions which you determine will produce good tone. The lengths will then vary accordingly.

After the bars are tuned to your satisfaction, find the nodes. This is done by measuring in 22.5% of the total length from the ends. A meter stick and a pocket calculator will be helpful here since it will spare you the pain of converting all those tenths and hundredths to their fractional equivalents. Or use the chart on page 199. At the nodal points glue a small strip of ¼-inch thick neoprene which you should be able to find at any store selling wetsuits or scuba diving equipment, or at any well-stocked hardware store. Or you can use weather-stripping or ensolite which is often sold as sleeping pads for backpacking. Any old foam rubber will do in a pinch.

The instrument can now be set on the floor or a table and played on the ends with a pair of mallets 7 to 8 inches long made from ¾-inch diameter dowel.

One typical amadinda melody which was passed on to us by Gary Griffith is as follows. Think of your notes being numbered from 1 to 5, with 1 the lowest and 5 the highest. Using the same amadinda, two players sit opposite each other.

One plays this pattern over and over in an even rhythm: 521,521,521....The other player enters right after the first person has played a 1 and plays 434, 332, 434, 422, with each note coming *exactly* in between the notes of player number one.

This technique is known as hocketing where each person plays a particular melodic or rhythmic idea over and over and it fits in and around the other parts. And it is a combination of these many separate parts fitting together that produces a musical whole greater than the sum of its parts. No one is in anyone else's way. Each separate musical identity merges into a sense of the whole. Some medieval musical forms are based on this concept, as is much of the music of Africa and Latin America.

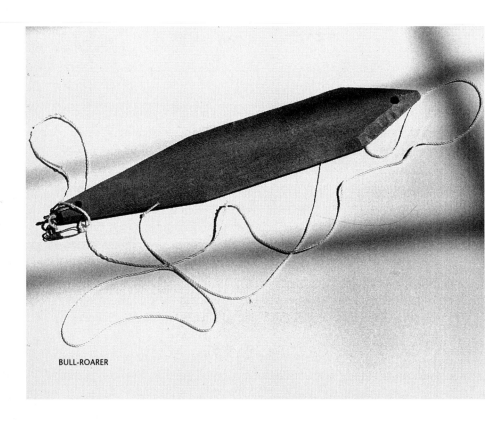

BULL-ROARER

BULL-ROARER

This instrument may have had its origins as a kind of sling for hunting, and if so would be one of the few instruments designed to be a weapon. However, if you get mad enough, most of the instruments in this book can be thrown at the enemy or the mirror or whatever. The Japanese shakuhachi flute was thought to have been used as a weapon in self-defense during the samurai times. But of course it wasn't invented for that purpose.

In the case of the bull-roarer, perhaps some early hunter was swinging the appropriately shaped piece of wood around his head aiming at some unsuspecting bird perched in a tree when the wood began to hum, frightened the bird away, and the hunter, while out his lunch, at least had a new instrument on his hands for his efforts.

All you need is a small piece of wood say 3 by 12 by $^3/_8$ inches thick, a long piece of sturdy string—use a coreless braid nylon to be extra safe—and a metal swivel available wherever fishing gear is sold. Cut or carve you wood into the general shape of the illustration, attach screw eye, swivel, string (do use a secure knot), and you are ready to swing. If the sound doesn't appear immediately, try reversing the direction or speed, and check to see that the cord isn't tangled. The board should spin around its axis while moving around your head. Varying the speed will also change the sound. For added beauty you may wish to carve decorations in the wood as is the custom in the South Sea Islands where this instrument is often used as part of the fertility and puberty ceremonies.

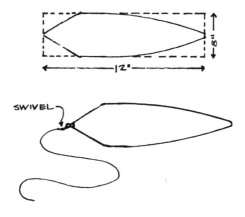

RECO-RECO

There are versions of this appropriately named instrument (pronounced hecku-hecku, which is how it sounds) in almost every non-European culture. It's unfortunate that in building a modern industrialized civilization, Europe and the United States have generally neglected community music and the basic instruments necessary for its enjoyment. What we have instead are highly refined string, wind, brass, and keyboard instruments, all of which are designed for classical music and are often too difficult to play to be used for homemade music.

Not so the reco-reco. Easy to make, easier to play. The reco-reco can be built by taking a 12 to 18-inch section of bamboo about 1 to 2 inches in diameter and sawing a section of it into ridges with a depth of $^1/_4$ inch or a bit less. If bamboo is not available, try it on an oblong gourd or a piece of 2-inch diameter plastic pipe. Space the cuts at least $^1/_8$-inch apart. Less than that and they will crack and break. To make your reco-reco double as a wood block, cut a slit in the sides, as shown:

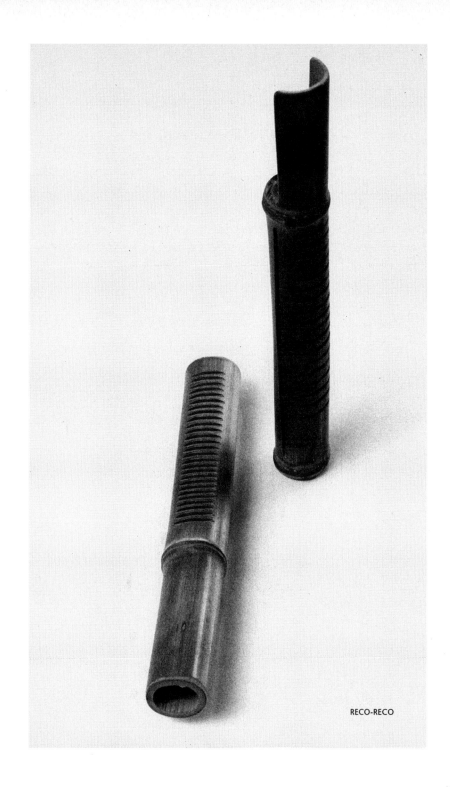

RECO-RECO

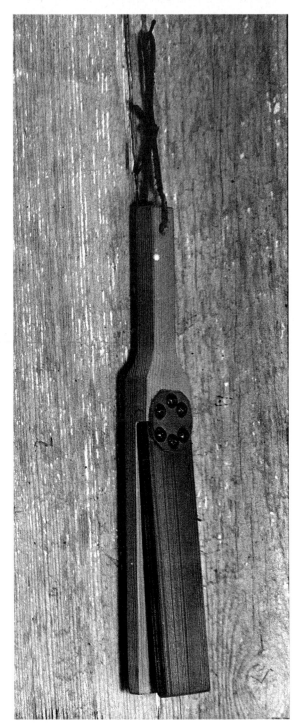

THE SLAPSTICK

THE SLAPSTICK

Having been born after the vaudeville era, we never understood the derivation of the phrase "slapstick humor" until we saw one of these. A version of the slapstick called P'ai pan is used in Asian orchestras and introduces different sections of the music being performed.

At most lumberyards, you can obtain $1/2$-inch pine known as drawer-stock. If unavailable use $1/2$-inch plywood. A 4 by 16-piece should be sufficient. Cut it into three pieces: 2 by 16 inches, 2 by 9 inches, and 2 by 2 inches. The length, of course, is somewhat arbitrary. You might want a great bodacious slapstick 2 to 3 feet long to make sure that everyone laughs when you crack a joke. Or you might want to make it for your child and adjust the dimensions accordingly. But for starters, here is an average size slapstick.

Glue and nail A to C. Box nails or any small nails are suitable. We used Atlas $3/4$-inch bright 18 gauge steel wire nails. Now nail a small leather hinge onto A and B. If you are a strict vegetarian, canvas or a metal hinge will do.

Cut off the excess wood from the handle to a size that fits comfortably in your hand, sanding it a little to take off the rough edges.

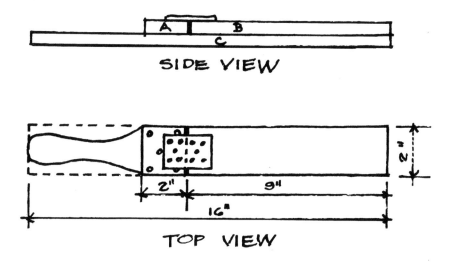

SIDE VIEW

TOP VIEW

SHEKERE

SHEKERE

Pronounced sheck-er-ā This is a gourd rattle typically used in African and Latin American music. If you enjoy gardening, you might try to grow your own gourds. Or they can be obtained from The Gourd Factory, Box 55311, Stockton, CA 95205. If you write them specify this general shape.

Begin by cutting off an inch or two from the top leaving a hole no bigger than 2¹/₂ inches. We cut ours with a hole saw attached to a drill press, but a sabre saw or a keyhole saw will be adequate. Scrape out the excess pith from the inside and put a protective coat or two of varathane on the outside.

We were given a large supply of metal pull-chain—the linked balls used to connect bathtub stoppers. And this served our purpose wonderfully. Using the pull chain, we made a collar around the neck of the gourd, then, with 18 gauge copper wire, wired vertical strings to another collar on the bottom. The strands were spaced 2 to 3 inches apart.

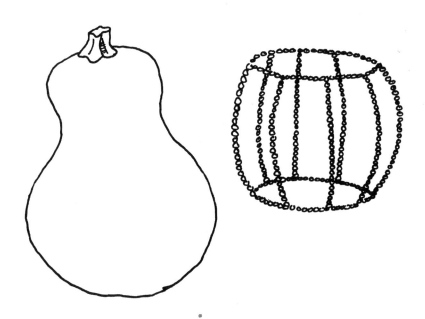

Metal bathroom chain this size may be difficult to come by. So if you are not averse to bead table work, try the following: Tie a cord collar loosely around the neck of your gourd. Around the collar, spaced evenly apart, loop from 10 to 30 3-foot long thin cords so that 18-inch lengths hang down. A coreless braid nylon fishing line or a heavier braided cotton thread works nicely. How many of these cords you choose to attach depends partly on the size of your gourd, partly on how loud you want it to be, and partly on how patient you are in doing this kind of meticulous work.

Next, you will need a supply of beads. Count on using at least 10 per string—more or less depending on the above factors. Some shekeres have 60 beads, some have 600. Take two beads, thread them on two adjacent strings that aren't part of the same loop, and slide them up to the collar. Tie a knot beneath. Repeat this process, going all the way around the gourd, then start a new row. Make sure all the knots are tied the same distance apart. You may want to leave a row or more without beads.

When you finally reach the bottom you can draw all the strings together and tie them off in a single knot. Or you may want to attach them to another collar on the bottom, which will leave you space in the center of the bottom to hit the gourd for additional effect.

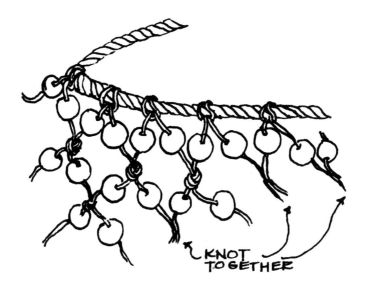

KNOT
TOGETHER

AN ORGAN PIPE

For the fun of it we built an organ pipe powered by that amazing source of wind and hot air—the human lungs. With some minor adjustments it can also be converted into a large and lethargic slide whistle.

The principle behind the organ pipe and, for that matter, the whistle, the flute and pan pipe as well, is this: if one takes a stream of air and sends it across an edge so as to split the stream, in the process of splitting it will create vibrations which are called edge tones. The edge tones in turn excite the columns of air inside whatever the edge is part of—flute, pipe, whistle, beer bottle, etc. If you change the volume of air in the container by the use of finger holes you will produce different notes.

To get a good tone out of a flute requires a bit of practice in order to properly direct the right amount of air at the right angle to the edge of the whole. With a whistle, organ pipe, recorder, or any of what are known as fipple flutes, the instrument is constructed so as to guide the stream of air towards an appropriately positioned edge which splits the air correctly and voilà—the note.

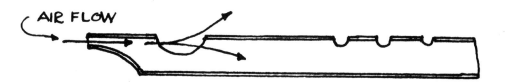

AIR FLOW

ORGAN PIPE

50

The following plans for an organ pipe will give you the basic proportions to construct them in other sizes. If you want to explore further, read *The Art of Organ Making* by Ashdown Audsley.

Glue and nail together three sides of a rectangular box whose inside measurement is 3 inches square. We used ⁵/₁₆-inch redwood 28 ³/₈ inches long. At one end of the box make a chamber 3 by 3 by 3 inches using two blocks ³/₄-inch thick. The inside block is 3 by 2 ¹⁵/₁₆ by ³/₄ inches and its top is angled as shown. The mouth block has a ⁵/₈-inch hole drilled in its center.

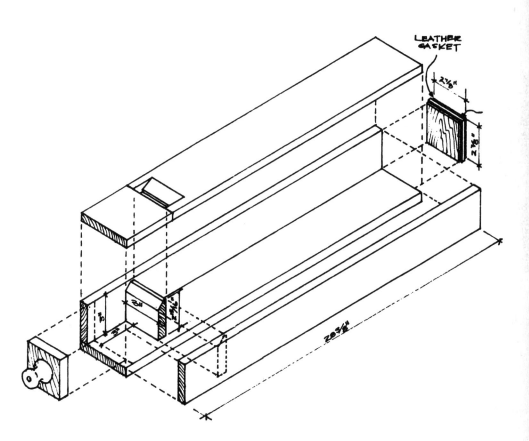

Cover the chamber with a piece 4½ by 3⅝ inches. Now, select a top 23⅝ by 3⅝ inches. At one end chisel out a ¾ by 3-inch opening. This will create a 1-inch lip sloping upwards as shown.

The other end piece is a removable adjustable stopper 2⅞ inches square and ⅝-inch thick with a thin leather gasket glued around the perimeter to ensure a tight fit. A handle, turned on a lathe, or a short length of dowel is attached to the stopper. A similarly turned mouthpiece is glued to the blow hole at the other end of the pipe, though the mouthpiece is not essential.

Options include building an armature to the stopper which allows it to be moved back and forth while the pipe is being played. Also, finger holes can be drilled into the top of the pipe to increase the number of possible notes.

WILLOW WHISTLE

The willow whistle is one of the all-time classic homemade musical instruments, with variations of it found in many non-arid sections of the world. The only ingredients needed for this simplest of flutes is a knife, a length of willow, and a little patience.

Willows are generally shrubs with many trunks and rather slender branches. The bark is smooth and grey-green, the leaves are slick and shiny, often a bright yellow green. The leaves tend to be narrow and 3 to 5 inches longer than they are wide. There are about 100 species of willow all over North America and they are found along rivers, streams, lakes, and other waters. If you can't find them, then look for any tree that has relatively straight branches, smooth bark, and sufficient sap between the bark and the wood. You must be able to separate the two without injuring either.

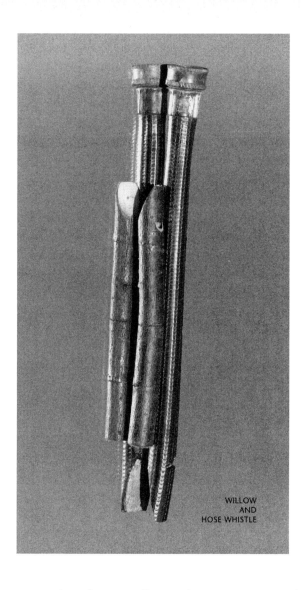

WILLOW
AND
HOSE WHISTLE

Once you've found your willow, select a piece around 6 inches long with a diameter equal to your forefinger or larger. Half of its length must be free from branches, nubs, or imperfections. Take your knife and cut through the bark around the circumference at the halfway point on your stick. Now make the cut for the mouthpiece about $^1/_4$-inch from the top as shown. Cut at an angle of about 45°. Next cut the notch for the air hole an inch from the end as shown.

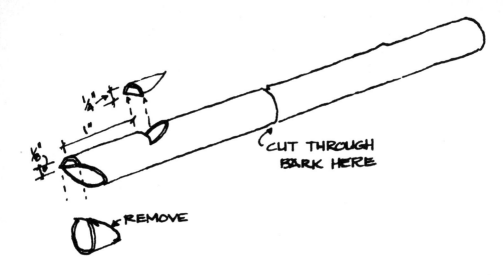

CUT THROUGH
BARK HERE

REMOVE

Now, carefully holding the knife by the blade, gently hammer around the circumference of the playing half of the wood, being careful not to rupture the bark. You are trying to loosen the bark from the wood so that it will slide off the end of the stick intact. After you have tapped gently around the entire surface of that half, try carefully twisting the bark to see if it breaks loose from the wood. If you twist too hard you may tear the bark and have to throw the stick away, so do it lightly and firmly. If nothing budges,

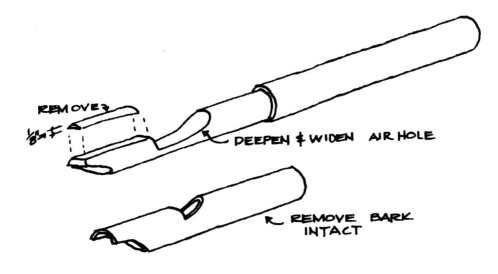

REMOVE

DEEPEN & WIDEN AIR HOLE

REMOVE BARK INTACT

54

resume your tapping, paying particular attention to the areas where there are imperfections in the wood. Now twist again. If it doesn't break loose try wedging the blunt edge of your knife blade into the slit and using a little lateral leverage. If this fails, tap some more. Eventually you will either succeed or damage the bark and have to try another piece. We've tried rubbing the bottom of a spoon around the bark as a means of loosening it, and you might give that a try.

When you do at last succeed (and it really may be no problem at all), whittle 1/8-inch from the mouthpiece as shown. Next deepen and lengthen the air hole. Slip the wood core back into the bark and blow. It might bring over all the dogs in the neighborhood. Then again it might not.

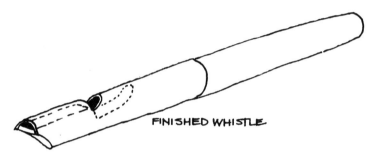

FINISHED WHISTLE

So you live in the city and don't have any nearby streams to find willow, and wouldn't know what it looks like if you did. Here's an alternative—the city dweller's version. Take any piece of hose that has at least six inches which aren't cracked or split, and a piece of dowel of a size which will fit tightly into the hose. Now follow the willow whistle instructions. First insert the dowel into the hose. Then use a saw to cut the mouthpiece angle and air hole notch. After finishing the shaping of the wood, you should glue it in. This will ensure that the fit is air-tight and make it easier to blow.

Should you want to make a hose whistle that's really a fipple flute, merely cut the insert as illustrated, glue it into the length of hose (it should be at least 8 inches long) and then punch 5 or 6 holes into the hose.

Or you can make a poot whistle by taking a slightly narrower piece of dowel and sticking it in the bottom of the flute and sliding it in and out.

SCALES

Before we proceed further, let's take a look at scales and how they are constructed. The scales for the instruments in this book are usually based on the system to which pianos are tuned—known as equal temperament. Or to those who chafe against the restrictions of equal temperament, well-tampered tuning. For in order to play harmony on a keyboard instrument and to move from one tonal center to another, certain compromises in tuning have to be made to allow the instrument to be "sort of" in tune in all the keys. This has created a musical aberration that is well suited to European harmonic demands, as Bach so beautifully demonstrated in his music "The Well-Tempered Clavier." He wrote it in part to show off the equal temperament system to best advantage. But for most of the rest of the world, harmony—or at least modulation—is not a primary concern in music. And so other cultures have intuitively gravitated toward scales that have more mathematically and musically exact ratios.

We use the tempered scale in this book only because it is more common in the West and it is what you will end up with as a reference scale if you tune to a pitch pipe or a piano. But as your ear becomes more perceptive, you may find that you want to use more acoustically precise tunings.

If you wish to play music that doesn't modulate, tuning an instrument by using simple ratios will make the sound more harmonically pure. The ratios represent the relationship between the frequencies of different notes in a scale—in this case the first or fundamental note and the succeeding notes. Thus a 4/3 ratio is one in which one note vibrates four times to every three vibrations of the note to which it is being compared. So if your fundamental is A, vibrating at 440 cycles per second (cps), the note with a 4/3 ratio above A will then vibrate at 586.66 cps—or 440 multiplied by four and the result divided by three.

Here are several different scales that you may wish to explore. A monochord and/or an oscilloscope are of great help in accurately tuning by ratios. The scales are given with their ratios and their frequencies based on A-220 cps. You may choose any other note as your fundamental 1/1. The ratios will remain the same in relationship to the note.

A DIATONIC MAJOR SCALE							
A	B	C#	D	E	F#	G#	A
1/1	55/49	63/50	578/433	433/289	37/22	185/98	2/1
220	246.94	277.18	293.66	329.63	369.99	415.30	440

Compare the complex tempered ratios above with the simple ratios of Just Tuning:

A SCALE BASED ON JUST INTONATION

1/1	9/8	5/4	4/3	3/2	5/3	15/8	2/1
220	247.5	275	293.33	330	366.66	412.5	440

THREE PENTATONIC SCALES

A scale similar to some found in African music:

1/1	9/8	4/3	3/2	5/3	2/1
220	247.5	293.33	330	366.66	440

A scale similar to the blues scale of Afro-American music:

1/1	6/5	4/3	3/2	9/5	2/1
220	264	293.33	330	396	440

One of the most common scales on the planet. Similar to the pentatonic scale found in country and western music:

1/1	9/8	5/4	3/2	5/3	2/1
220	247.5	275	330	366.66	440

You can, of course, make up your own tunings using various ratios. Don't let the conditioning of equal temperament lead you to believe that other scales are out of tune. By allowing your ears time to grow accustomed to new tunings, you will discover that each has its own individual charm.

If you wish to go further with scales, refer to the books by Harry Partch and Lou Harrison listed in the bibliography. They are very persuasive about the virtues of ratio tuning and just intonation.

RESONATORS

Almost any vibrating object enjoys having a resonator in close proximity. Stringed instruments would be barely audible if it weren't for the body to which the strings are attached. Marimbas and vibraphones have resonator tubes under the keys to strengthen their sound. And the loudspeakers in your stereo system would be softspeakers if they weren't enclosed in a box that has been carefully designed by acoustical engineers to give them maximum amplification.

The resonator is in effect a container of air set in motion by the vibration from the instrument of which it is a part. Optimally, the air in the resonator vibrates at the same speed as the object that has been struck.

Resonators can range from the beautifully crafted bodies of the violins of Cremona to oral cavities used by the Ainus of Japan who sing into each other's mouths in order to produce stronger and more unique sounds.

For our purposes, we will be concerned with constructing tubular resonators to enhance the tone and volume of glass, metal, and wood marimbas, and plastic and skin head drums.

There is a formula for determining what length resonator with a closed end is necessary to produce any given note.

$$L = \frac{C}{4F}$$

L is the length of the resonator, C is the velocity of sound at average room temperature—this will be 1130 feet per second, or 13,560 inches per second. This is divided by 4 times the frequency of the given note. For example, if you have a bar that produces the note "A" vibrating at 110 cycles per second, multiply 110 by 4 and divide the result into 13,560. The result is a resonator length of 30.82 inches. Now you need to make what is known as the "open end correction." Subtract 0.29 of the inside diameter of the pipe. If you have 2-inch pipe, you will subtract 2 x 0.29 or 0.58 of an inch from the quotient, leaving you 30.24 or 30 1/4 inches when converted to a fractional equivalent.

Resonators can be made out of many kinds of materials and in many shapes. Some African and Central American marimbas use gourds. Indonesian gamelans use bamboo. American vibraphones use aluminum. If sealed properly, rectangular wooden boxes work well. But for ease of assembly we've found that the material of choice is acrylonitrile butadiene styrene tubing (commonly called ABS pipe and used for sewer pipe), though PVC pipe will work almost as well. This was suggested to us by Mel McBride, who builds marvelous calliopes and marimbas.

It is important that your resonator be airtight. Cut out plywood circles and glue them to one end of the pipe, using ABS cement, or glue in temporary caps. Add an extra coat around the seam after the first coat has dried so that the seal is complete. Don't stint on the glue.

At the top of each resonator, attach an ABS coupling that has been cut in half. This serves not only to support the resonator when it is placed in its stand, but also works as a tuning device. By sliding it back and forth, you can lengthen or shorten the pipe and thus alter the pitch.

You also might want to experiment with the buzz tone that some of the marimbas of Central America and Africa have built into their resonators. A small hole is drilled in to the gourds and then covered with a thin membrane. This buzzes when the note is struck to add yet another element to the sound.

For those of you who hated math in school and would rather not take advantage of the wizardry of pocket calculators, we have prepared a chart of typical resonator lengths and the note they will produce given an average room temperature. This will be convenient if your instruments are tuned to an equal tempered scale. However, if you are more adventurous in your tunings, then you will need to use the $L = \dfrac{C}{4F}$ formula.

Equal-Temperament Diatonic Scale
RESONATOR LENGTHS
At Average Room Temperature

Note	Frequency	Length of Resonator Before "Open End Correction:" (Inches)	With "Open End Correction:"	
			4-inch Diameter Resonator	2-inch Diameter Resonator
E	659.26	5.14	4	$4^9/_{16}$
D	587.23	5.78	$4^5/_8$	$5^3/_{16}$
C	523.25	6.48	$5^5/_{16}$	$6^7/_8$
B	493.88	6.87	$5^{11}/_{16}$	$6^5/_{16}$
A	440	7.70	$6^9/_{16}$	$7^1/_8$
G	392.00	8.65	$7^1/_2$	$8^1/_{16}$
F	349.23	9.71	$8^9/_{16}$	$9^1/_8$
E	329.63	10.29	$9^1/_8$	$9^{11}/_{16}$
D	293.66	11.55	$10^3/_8$	11
C	261.63	12.96	$11^{13}/_{16}$	$12^3/_8$
B	246.94	13.73	$12^9/_{16}$	$13^1/_8$
A	220	15.40	$14^1/_4$	$14^{13}/_{16}$
G	196.00	17.30	$16^1/_8$	$16^3/_4$
F	174.61	19.42	$18^1/_4$	$18^{13}/_{16}$
E	164.81	20.57	$19^3/_8$	20
D	146.83	23.10	$21^7/_8$	$22^1/_2$
C	130.81	25.92	$24^3/_4$	$25^5/_{16}$
B	123.47	27.46	$26^5/_{16}$	$26^7/_8$
A	110	30.82	$29^5/_8$	$30^1/_4$
G	97.99	34.60	$33^7/_{18}$	34
F	87.30	38.83	$37^{11}/_{16}$	$38^1/_4$
E	82.40	41.14	40	$40^9/_{16}$
D	73.41	46.18	45	$45^5/_8$
C	65.40	51.83	$50^{11}/_{16}$	$51^1/_4$
B	61.73	54.92	$53^3/_4$	$54^5/_{16}$
A	55	61.64	$60^1/_2$	$61^1/_{16}$

WOOD & METAL

REDWOOD MARIMBA

REDWOOD MARIMBA

Few moments in instrument building are more satisfying than taking an ordinary-sounding piece of wood or metal, placing it over a correctly tuned resonator, and hearing that ordinary sound grow in volume, richness, and duration. This is not to downgrade unresonated instruments. They possess a sweetness and purity entirely their own. Yet the difference can be compared to that between a solo voice and a unison choir.

The following two instruments and the crystal marimba can all be constructed without resonators, but you will be well rewarded if you make the effort to build a set. In fact, if you plan to make all three, you can save time by doing the resonators in triplicate. Use 2-inch diameter pipe and follow the instructions and measurements on pages 58-60.

Here is the design for a diatonic marimba made of redwood. Find the best piece of 1x3 you can, or rip down to 1 x 3 whatever the next larger size is available. Dry, clear heart, vertical grain, quarter-sawn. That should be a chant that you use whenever you enter a lumberyard in search of wood for instrument tops. Our thirteen bars were cut into these dimensions, giving the notes F below middle C to D above second C.

20″	15 $^9/_{16}$″	13 $^7/_8$″	11 $^7/_8$″
19 $^3/_{16}$″	14 $^1/_4$″	12 $^3/_4$″	11 $^3/_4$″
17 $^7/_8$″	14 $^1/_8$″	11 $^{15}/_{16}$″	11 $^1/_{16}$″
16 $^1/_2$″			

If you use a wood other than redwood (spruce, for example), your measurements may be somewhat different but proportional. Hardwoods can also be used with the resulting tone being brighter and not as warm.

Next, find the nodes for each block. Since you will be carving out much of the wood underneath the blocks, the nodes will be 20% of the length from each end rather than the usual 22.5%.

Mark the nodes and then, starting ³/₈-inch in from each node, cut away an arch between them, leaving about one-half the thickness of the block. This can be done on a joiner, or with a band saw, sabre saw, belt sander, or rasp. Now, fine tune the bars. To lower the pitch, file away a bit of wood from underneath; to raise it file off wood from the end. We used a stroboscope tuning device and tuned our marimbas to a diatonic tempered scale beginning at F 174.6 cps. You may wish to tune yours to a different scale or to a ratio scale tuning such as described on pages 56-57. A monochord and/or an oscilloscope is useful for this procedure. However, if you aren't concerned with pinpoint accuracy, then you can tune yours using a pitch pipe for comparison.

Now for your stand. Here is one simple and effective design:

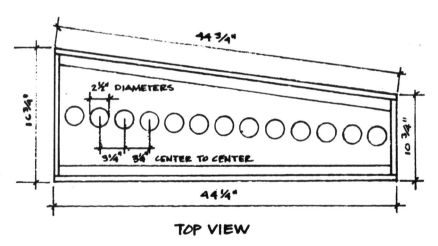

TOP VIEW

The top is made from ¹/₈-inch doorskin plywood reinforced with cross braces. You can use thicker plywood or hard masonite and it will be stronger, but it will also be heavier and more expensive. The sides are made from 1x4 redwood (though plywood will

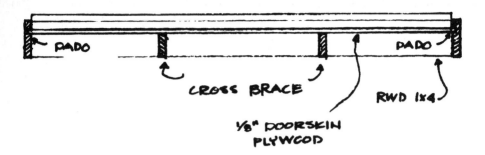

DADO   CROSS BRACE   RWD 1x4

⅛" DOORSKIN
PLYWOOD

work just fine) and can be butted or mitred together (butt joints are relatively strong, mitre joints are pretty). To suspend the top, plow out a groove in the sides ⅛-inch wide by ¼-inch deep with a dado blade ½-inch from the top. Or use cleats to support it from underneath.

The holes for the resonators are 2½ inches in diameter and 3¼ inches apart on center. They can be most easily cut out with an electric drill using a hole saw, but a sabre saw or key hole saw will also suffice.

To support the bars we glued down two 1¼ by 1½-inch wooden rails along the top. Into one rail had been pounded 20d nails with their ends clipped and the remaining exposed section covered with a sleeve of surgical or other rubber tubing. The nails were positioned to fit on either side of the bars to prevent them from moving laterally.

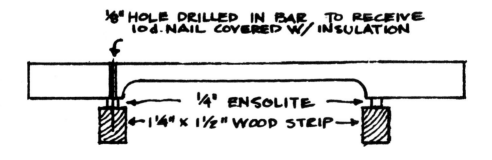

⅛" HOLE DRILLED IN BAR TO RECEIVE
10d. NAIL COVERED W/ INSULATION

¼" ENSOLITE

← 1¼" x 1½" WOOD STRIP →

In the other rail, 10d nails were pounded, the heads clipped off, and the remainder covered with a sleeve of thin plastic tubing stripped off of insulated wire. These nails were positioned so as to fit into a $1/8$-inch hole drilled into one of the nodes of each bar.

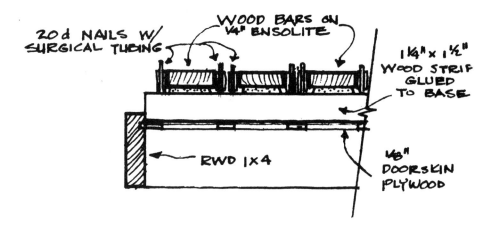

Additionally, at the underside of each bar at the node was glued a $1/4$-inch wide strip of ensolite. However, ensolite often has a tendency to compress under any significant weight and lose some of its resilience. You can avoid this by using neoprene or any other sturdy foam.

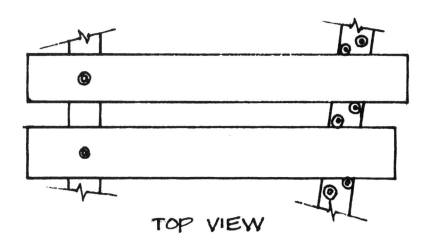

TOP VIEW

The legs are 1 3/8-inch dowels 34 inches long. They fit into ferrules made out of exhaust pipe with a fender washer welded to the top end and bolts welded to the side in order to attach it to the stand. Vertical legs are easier to attach but they are not quite as stable, so we angled ours a bit.

Redwood marimbas sound best when played with superball beaters or other soft mallets.

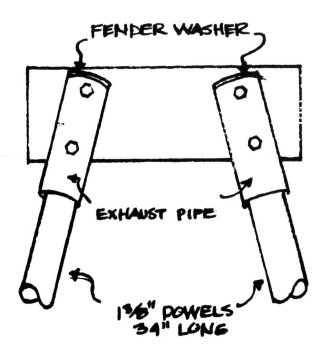

FENDER WASHER

EXHAUST PIPE

1⅜" DOWELS
34" LONG

TUBELODIOUS

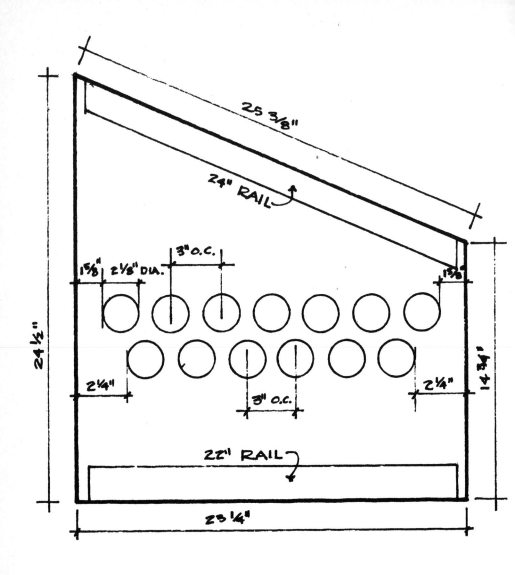

The Tubelodious is the easiest to make of the marimbas, and cheapest, too! Its notes are produced by 1/2-inch thinwall electrical metallic tubing (E.M.T.), commonly called conduit. This is relatively inexpensive material and can obtained at electrical supply shops and large hardware stores. You will need around 30 feet for this project. Diameters larger than 1/2-inch can also be used but they produce a different pitch and you will have to adjust your resonator lengths accordingly. Using a pipe cutter or a hacksaw, cut the following lengths:

31 3/16″	25 3/8″	19 7/16″
29 3/8″	23 7/8″	18 7/16″
27 11/16″	22 9/16″	17 13/16″
26 1/8″	21 7/8″	16 15/16″
	20 5/8″	

These sizes should produce a diatonic major tempered scale in the key of C at F 174.6. Fine tuning is achieved by cutting or filing off the ends to raise the pitch. If you raise it too much it may be easier to use that tube for the next higher note and cut a new one. If need be, nuts and washers bolted to the end of the tubing will lower the pitch.

Find the nodes—22.5% of the distance from the end—and drill a hole through one of the nodes so that the tube can be suspended securely over the resonators. The appropriate resonator sizes are found on page 60.

The stand is of similar materials as the preceding marimba stands, but with dimensions as shown in the drawing at left.

The tubes are secured in the same fashion as the wood marimba, with a plastic covered nail coming up through the hole in the bar. At the other node there is a similarly covered supporting nail on either side of the bar.

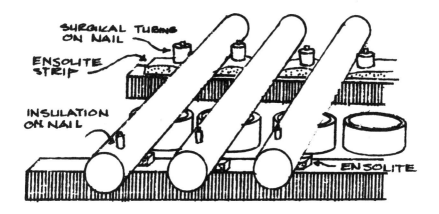

SURGICAL TUBING
ON NAIL

ENSOLITE
STRIP

INSULATION
ON NAIL

ENSOLITE

THUMB PIANO

The African thumb piano—also known as the sanza, kalimba, or mbira—creates some of the world's most beautiful and innocent sounds. Simple and pure, it has a timelessness that less repetitive, more complex instruments can never duplicate. And it is fairly easy to build and even easier to play. In fact, anyone playing it can make Perfect Music.

In our town there was a group of musicians meeting together on Thursday nights a few years ago under the direction of Max Hartstein. They were an offshoot of his 25th Century Music Ensemble, and they were dedicated to playing what Max calls Perfect Music. As he puts it, "No one can play imperfect music because all the wrong notes have already been played."

Anyone could show up on a Thursday evening and play any instrument in any way they wanted to. Both professional musicians and novices played regularly. One described a typical session during which Max suggested that they play a blues in F. The musicians who knew how to play the blues in the key of F launched off into the tune. And everyone else who didn't know how to play anything but Perfect Music played along the way they felt—including the kid who had brought along his harmonica tuned to the key of G, and the person who was beating on some metal space sculptures, and someone else who had just picked up a saxophone for the first time and was honking away on it. The person who described it to us said, "It's as if the people who could actually play the blues in F became a big ship on the sonic ocean of Perfect Music (a blend of monotone and cacophony). They could always jump into the ocean and swim around for a while knowing that the blues-in-F-ship was still there as a means of returning to port."

That is what Perfect Music is about. It's an attitude towards making music that permits anything. One does not have to be labeled a "musician" to enjoy the experience of playing with sound for its own sake.

The thumb piano is an excellent way to enjoy Perfect Music. Children can play it. If it is tuned properly, anything sounds nice on it. And the masters of the instrument from Africa produce lovely cascades of sound both complex and rhythmically demanding. The simplest version we've run across is an mbira from Ghana. To make one you will need an oval sardine tin, a thin piece of clear, soft wood (pine or redwood or a cedar shingle), a strip of tin can, some tacks, and the tines from a metal rake or a short length of $3/32$-inch piano wire, available at larger hardware stores. It is made as follows:

Go out and buy the largest oval tin of sardines you can find. Make yourself a sardine sandwich and while enjoying it, read the rest of these instructions. If you are a vegetarian, give the sardines

to your cat; if you are catless, given them to a fish-eating friend. If you are friendless, try organic gardening and bury the sardines with the corn you plant. If you have no corn, turn to the next section.

Next select a piece of wood for the top ¼-inch thick, or use a cedar shingle. If you can't find any wood that thin, plane a piece down to the proper size by hand or with a jointer. Then trace an outline of the tin can on the wood and cut out the top to your thumb piano with a sabre or coping saw or pocket knife. Make sure that the edge of the blade is on the outside of the outline, rather than the inside.

If you are unable to locate a metal rake for the notes (they often turn up without their handles at garage sales), use piano wire. On an anvil, chunk of railroad tie, or any other hard metal surface, flatten out five pieces of the wire approximately 3½ to 4 inches long. You should hammer them down as thin as you can without cracking them. They will probably be somewhere between .018 and .032 inches thick, about the thickness of the cardboard at the end of writing tablets. Or you can check with an automotive feeler gauge for accuracy. The easiest way to cut your wire to the proper length after you have hammered down a piece is to put it in a vise, bend it over, and whack on the bend with a hammer. Or pound it over a sharp corner. Trying to use wire cutters may damage the cutting edges. For ease of playing and for aesthetic appeal, you can make your tongues into three different sizes: two pieces 3¾ inches, two at 3½ inches, and one 4-inch piece.

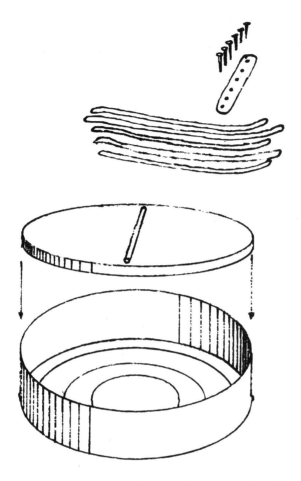

Next cut out a rectangular piece of tin can or other lightweight metal $2^1/2$ inches long by $^1/2$-inch wide. The tin can be cut with old scissors or tin snips. Place this over your five tongues and tap holes in it. Then nail it to the oval piece of wood a quarter of the distance from one end. Nail it with tacks or wire nails with your anvil, or anvil substitute, underneath so that the tips of the tacks are slightly crushed back into the wood to give a firmer grip. If you're using wire nails, bend them at right angles to the wood grain. Remove the tongues.

Now comes the final shaping of the wooden top. What you are trying to do is to have the top fit into the sardine can as snugly as possible—perhaps even flush with the edge. To do this, bevel the sides of the piece using a surform rasp and sandpaper. This is a little tricky since you don't want to file down too much or the top will drop through. So bevel a little bit at a time and keep checking till it fits tightly and evenly. Glue with epoxy for additional security.

Before inserting the tongues you may want to smooth off the ends a bit with an electric grinder or sandpaper. Nothing like bloody thumbs to take the fun out of playing. Also, buffing the tongues will bring out a nice shine.

Now put the tongues into place and cut one more piece of round piano wire 2¹/₂ inches long for your bridge. Place this under the tongue about ¹/₄-inch from the brace. A piece of thicker wire or a section of coat hanger inserted behind the wire will make it easier for you to get the bridge close to the brace.

You can tune your mbira by sliding the tongues towards the bridge or away from it to raise or lower the pitch. Needlenose pliers are a help with this if the tongues don't move easily. Watch out that they don't slip while you are pushing and ram into the wooden face. Tune to whatever sounds nice to you, or try tuning it to one of the pentatonic scales listed on page 57. Excellent examples of thumb piano playing can be found in the CD *Zimbabwe–Soul of Mibra*.

MARIMBULAS AND RJONS

MARIMBULA

Marimbulas and rjons are oversized versions of the thumb piano. The marimbula is of Afro-Cuban origin and is used for rhythm accompaniment. With its low tones, it sounds somewhat like a bass viol. It can be played either by hand or with the aid of large super-ball mallets.

To construct a marimbula, find or build a box sufficiently large and resonant to amplify the vibrations of five or six pieces of spring steel. The box can be a drawer, particularly if it is one of the older, less flimsy models. We built our box out of redwood, with a plywood bottom, and with dimensions of 9 by 18 by 27 inches. We chose this size for its visual proportions. As long as it's large enough, you can make it most any shape.

The sides are made from 1x10s. The top is three pieces of 1x8 18 inches long with a piece of 1x4 at each end, all glued together and then sanded down to a smooth finish. Always select for the tops of your instruments the best wood available. The better the grain and quality of the wood, the better the tone of the instrument—Reinhold's Thirty-seventh Law. If redwood is unavailable, or if you wish to be spared the problems of laminating (enough clamps, enough glue, enough time, and enough accuracy), then try using a piece of $^3/_8$ or $^1/_2$-inch hardwood plywood.

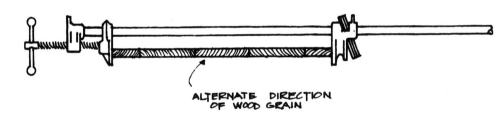

ALTERNATE DIRECTION
OF WOOD GRAIN

Tongues can be fashioned out of large electric hacksaw blades or any other kind of thin spring steel such as old hand saws. Cabinet scrapers, in 5 and 6-inch lengths, were what we used, cutting them into two sections each about $1^1/_2$ inches wide. This can be done with a saw, using an abrasive blade. Or, easier still, you can stick them in a vise, score them with a three-pointed file, and snap them off along the score mark.

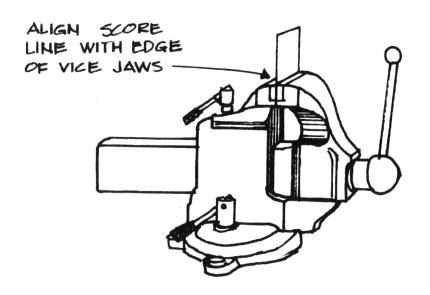

ALIGN SCORE
LINE WITH EDGE
OF VICE JAWS

The tongues are then suspended over two 12-inch pieces of ¼-inch diameter welding rod. This is held in place with ¼ by 2-inch hex-head bolts (called machine cap screws) through a ½ by 1 by 13-inch piece of walnut or other hardwood through the top of the marimbula into a similar piece of walnut glued to the underside of the top where the bolts are anchored by tee nuts. Two 1½-inch diameter holes are drilled into the top to increase sound dispersal.

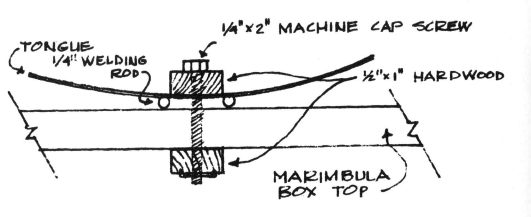

TONGUE
¼" WELDING ROD
¼"x2" MACHINE CAP SCREW
½"x1" HARDWOOD
MARIMBULA BOX TOP

The rjon is a medium-sized compromise between the extremes of a thumb piano and a marimbula. Ours is 9 1/2 by 12 by 2 1/8 inches deep with a plywood bottom, redwood sides, and a cedar shingle top.

The tongues are all discarded electric hacksaw blades of varying sizes with their teeth ground off. In a fashion similar to the marimbula, they are suspended over two 8 1/2-inch pieces of 3/8 by 1-inch walnut that is bolted onto the top and anchored with tee nuts in a similar piece of walnut immediately under the top. It is played in the same fashion as the marimbula: with fingers or superball mallets.

RJON

MONOCHORDS

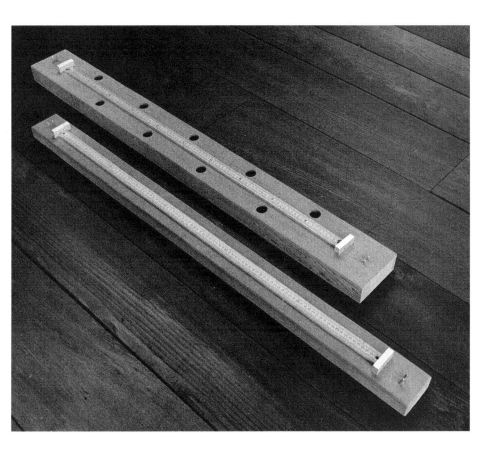

Most stringed instruments, from violins and guitars to pianos, are of such complex design that they are out of the realm of this book. However, we've chosen to give plans for two simple instruments that will connect you with some of the basic principles at work in the string family. They also have practical music value.

History has it that the monochord was invented by Pythagoras as a means of explaining musical ratios and scales. He designed it with only one string. But in the fourteenth century, as harmony developed, a second string was added to allow one note to be compared to another—the study of intervals.

Here is an elaboration of a primitive but effective monochord given to us by Ludwig V. B. Hinrichs. He had glued a yardstick to a 2x4 and passed two strings over bolted-down bridges. We substituted a meter stick for the yard stick and built a second version with a box resonator to amplify the tone.

If you want to make the simpler version, select a piece of 2x4 at least 48 inches long and free from warpage. Glue and nail the meter stick to the top. Construct two bridges, one for each end, using any dense material. We used aluminum bar stock 1/2 by 3/4 by 2 inches and drilled two holes in it for the strings to pass through. You could also use walnut or Lucite for the bridge. And the strings can either go through holes in or over the top of your bridge. At one end of the 2x4 drill two holes and insert pop rivets or nails 1/2-inch apart. These will anchor your strings.

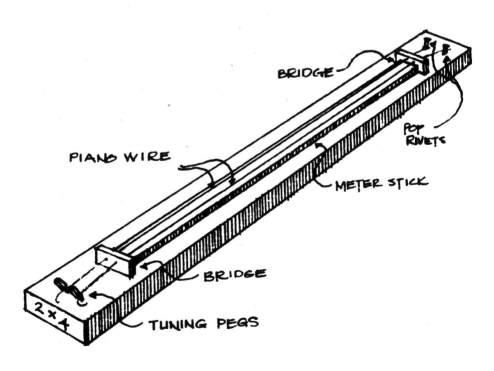

BRIDGE

POP RIVETS

PIANO WIRE

METER STICK

BRIDGE

2 x 4

TUNING PEGS

At the other end, drill holes for and insert two tuning pegs ⅛-inch in diameter—available at music stores and used for autoharps. The holes should be a hair smaller than the diameter of the pegs. Take two lengths of .010 to .014 piano wire, make a loop to fit over the pop rivet, pass the wire over the bridge and attach to the tuning pegs. These may be tuned by using either a tuning wrench, available from most music stores, or an adjustable crescent wrench.

For a resonated monochord, construct a box with the following dimensions:

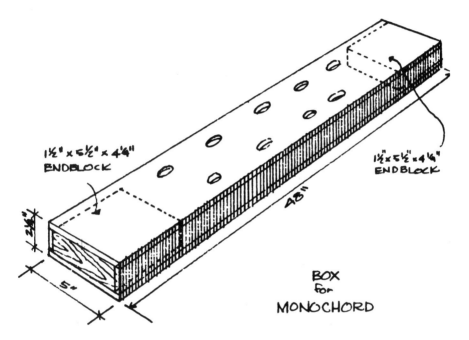

1½" × 5½" × 4'4" ENDBLOCK

1½" × 5½" × 4'4" ENDBLOCK

48"

2¾"

5"

BOX
for
MONOCHORD

We used ⅜-inch redwood paneling called La Honda in the trade. Spruce, of course, would be nice, but even thin plywood is sufficient. Glue the meter stick on top and set up bridges and strings in the same fashion as in the preceding instrument. Be sure your tuning pegs and pop rivets are inserted into the end blocks. If they slip under tension apply a little chalk to them before you stick them in.

To hear different scales or intervals, tune the strings to the same pitch. The string farthest from you will be a reference—the fundamental note. The other string can be varied in pitch by sliding the leading edge of a small bar of metal or other hard substance *lightly* along the top of the string. (Any significant deflection of the string downward will improperly alter the pitch.)

For example, when the edge is directed over the 50-mm mark you will hear a note vibrating at twice the speed of your reference note. This is commonly called the octave note. More accurately, it is referred to as a 2/1, indicating the vibration ratio between the two strings. If you sound the string at 66.6 mm you will get the note known as the fifth above the fundamental—a ratio of 3/2. Place your bar so that the body lies to the right of your point and pluck that part of the string lying to the left of the leading edge.

Try out some of the ratios listed in the section on scales. Simply divide the top number in the ratio into 100 mm and multiply the result by the bottom number.

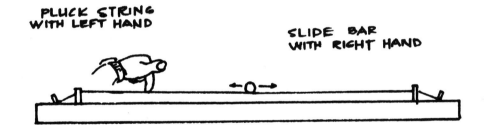

AEOLIAN HARP-ZITHER

The aeolian harp is not really a harp at all, but a box-resonated zither with ten or more strings of different diameters all tuned, at low tension, to the same note. It is placed outside or in a window, where the wind can pass by and set the strings in motion. It is relatively simple to make and of course effortless to play.

We built our first aeolian harp from plans drawn up by Dick Hughes. But while we were constructing it we saw ways to make modifications to the harp and thus make it more versatile—something we encourage you to do with any of the instruments in this book. Here are the dimensions:

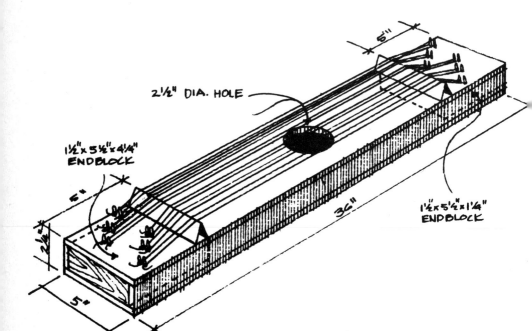

We used ³/₈-inch redwood La Honda paneling all around, but thin plywood sides and back would be adequate substitutes. If you choose to use the paneling you can smooth out the rough side on a jointer or plane it down, then sand it to your satisfaction. For our bridges, we used an aluminum tracking mechanism from sliding glass doors. A triangular length of hard wood, dense plastic, or hard metal would work just as well. One of our harp-zithers has two sets of bridges. One set is stationary, the other is a mini-bridge for each string. These are slightly higher than the stationary bridge and can be slid back and forth for secondary tuning purposes, much like the moveable bridges of a Japanese koto. Additionally, we made a set of small hammers out of bamboo so that the instrument

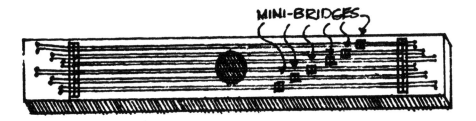

could be played like a santoor or hammered dulcimer. For strings, use assorted light gauge guitar strings or piano wire (.010 to .016 gauge) or unwound nylon guitar strings used for classical guitars.

COPPER MARACAS

Maracas are a must for Latin music and can be made out of a variety of materials. Reinhold came up with the idea for these toilet treasures, and not only are they pretty to behold, but they are extremely responsive with a nice, dry tone.

You can find copper tank floats in most any abandoned toilet, but chances are they will be corroded and funky. Since they are relatively inexpensive, it might be easier to buy them new at a hardware or plumbing supply store.

With a drill and a $^1/_8$ or $^5/_{32}$-inch bit, make a hole where the arm is usually threaded—doing it *carefully* so as not to damage the threads. Now pour in a handful of B.B.'s or shot for a loud tone, or use seeds for a softer, dry sound. As you pour in your shot or seeds, hold the float lightly and shake it to test it for the amount and tone you most like.

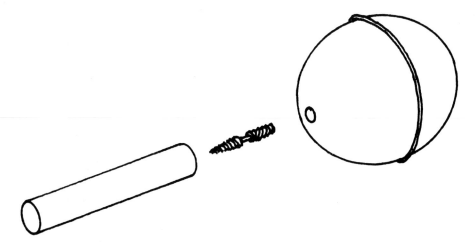

For handles, if you have access to a lathe, take a piece of 1$^1/_4$-inch stock and shape it. If there is no lathe, $^3/_4$ to 1-inch dowel about 4 inches long will suffice depending on the size of the hand that's holding it. The end can be chiseled or carved out to fit the shape of the float. Next, drill a small starter hole in the concave end of your handle and screw in a $^3/_{16}$-inch diameter "hanger bolt." These are the kind of screws that are bolt threaded on one end and screw threaded on the other. Now bolt the handle onto the float and you're ready to mambo.

THUNDERSHEETS &
WOBBLE BOARDS

Large pieces of flexible metal or thin, resilient woods can produce distinctive sounds similar to thunder or to the "boing, boing" sound heard in "Tie Me Kangaroo Down," the popular song of many years ago from Australia.

For a large thunder sheet we used a mahogany plywood doorskin—$\frac{1}{8}$-inch thick, with three plies. The size of this is a standard 3 by 7 feet, and, as the name suggests, it is used to sheath hollow or particle-board core doors. To play it, hold the sides and wave it slowly. This will produce a deep, rumbly sound.

Wobble boards utilize the same principle but are generally smaller and higher pitched. For one of these try a 10 by 36-inch piece of 26 gauge cold rolled or galvanized steel. This is commonly used to make gutters or down spouts and can be found at sheet metal shops. Handles for the wobble board will not only add a nice visual touch, but will make it easier to hold onto as you wobble about. Two pieces of 1x2 4 to 6 inches long nailed together at each end will do the trick. Or take a large dowel, cut it in half and bolt it on.

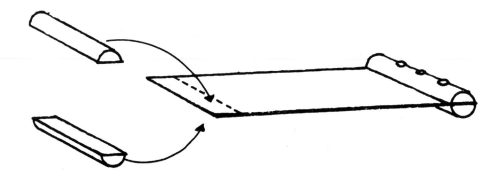

You may also wish to experiment with larger or smaller sizes to obtain different sound qualities. Or try making them out of thin masonite or sheets of plastic. And thunder sheets may be made out of the same galvanized metal as your wobble board. Take a piece 2 by 4 feet and bend it in one or more places to create multiple sounds. Bending this kind of metal is most easily done by clamping two boards along the end to be bent and then pressing the sheet back against the boards.

THUNDER SHEET

WELDING & OTHER HEAVY METAL MYSTERIES

Since we've already been presumptuous enough to try to reduce all woodworking knowledge to one section, we will brazenly try to do the same with welding. Of course, it can't be done. The best way to learn is to find someone with enough experience, patience, and time to guide you. Or try the adult education program in your community. It may offer classes in welding.

The real purpose of this section is to show you that the *basic* theoretical information and instructions can in fact be set down in a few pages. And perhaps this will encourage you to try learning the practical aspects from an experienced teacher. Welding skills are very useful tools to have not only for construction and shop work, but also for gadgeteering, sculpture, and instrument building. Many of the stands and some of the instrument designs in this book call for welding. There are always ways to circumvent the process, but few of the circumventions are as fast or as elegant. So if you've never had the urge to learn, perhaps this short introduction will put you in motion.

Although electric arc welding is common and quite easy, we will restrict ourselves to oxy-acetylene welding since it is easier for lightweight jobs. In this process, two gases are mixed together in correct proportions to produce a high temperature flame. The heat from the flame is then applied to the metals that are to be joined, a molten puddle is created, and the edges melt together and become one. Usually a welding rod called filler rod is used to strengthen the bond.

To weld, you will need a cylinder each of oxygen and acetylene with separate reducing regulators for both, hoses to carry the two gases to a torch, the torch, a tip for the torch or a cutting attachment depending on whether you will be welding or cutting, and a spark lighter that will ignite your gas. Additionally, you should have welding goggles and gloves, and a hat to avoid the possibility of a flaming hairdo.

OBSERVE THE FOLLOWING SAFETY PRECAUTIONS: Make sure your workspace is free from inflammables and away from flammables. Goggles should always be worn. Any observers should also wear goggles or avoid looking directly into the flame as it is very hard on one's eyes. Make sure there is adequate ventilation. Handle your cylinders carefully. They should be chained and bolted upright when in use. NEVER use oil or petroleum products on or in your welding equipment. Turn on the cylinder valves slowly to prevent damage to the regulators, and, as a precaution, stand to one side when opening the oxygen cylinder valve in case the gauge bursts. If you stop welding for more than a few minutes, close your cylinder valves. Should your torch ever do anything other than work properly, shut it off as quickly as you can. If you hear a squealing or hissing sound and see black smoke, the flame has flashbacked into your torch. Immediately shut off first your oxygen and then your acetylene. NEVER cut or weld anything that has been used to store combustibles or explosives. Don't use equipment that has any leaks. Turn off the torch unless it is in your hand. If you drink, don't drive, and don't weld either. Use your common sense. Always think safety.

Now that we have listed all the big bang fears, let's get a flame going. Select the proper tip for your work. In general the thinner the metal, the smaller the tip. Get your goggles situated on your head, above your eyes. Now, open up the valves on top of each tank. Set your oxygen regulator at 10 lbs. The oxygen tank is the big one with the green tube running to it. The regulator with its two gauges will be right above the tank. One gauge tells you how much pressure is in the tank, the other indicates the pressure of the gas leading to the torch. Now set your acetylene regulator at 5 lbs. Open up the secondary acetylene valve at the base of the torch handle (the one with the red hose leading to it) and check to make sure that your pressure still reads about 5 lbs. Then get your striker. Hold it an inch in front of your tip and, with the torch in one hand and the striker in the other, press the flint across the file with your thumb and flick it across the surface of the file. This is a little tricky, though once you get the hang of it, it will come automatically.

Okay, now once you have the acetylene lit, you should adjust the flame to where it is just in between a lazy flame and one with

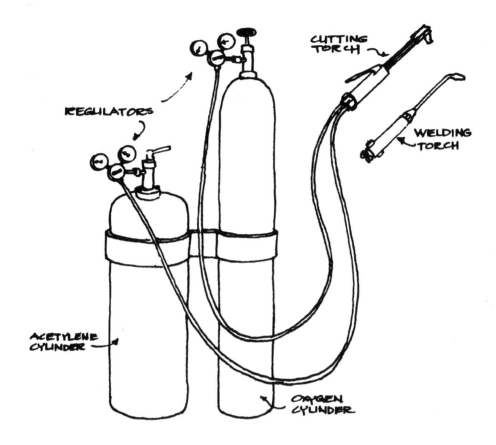

gusto—so call it an expectant flame. Using too little gas will cause the torch to pop (as will a dirty tip) and ignite inside the torch, in which case you will have to turn it off and start again. Now with the acetylene flame yellow-red, S-L-O-W-L-Y open up the oxygen valve adjacent to the acetylene valve. The expectant acetylene flame will turn blue and begin to roar. Your flame should now have three parts to it—see illustration. Adjust the oxygen flow so that the middle part, which is called the acetylene feather, merges with the smallest part, the white inner cone. This will give you what is called a neutral flame which will be used for most welding procedures. It is a 5 to 6-inch, tapered, reddish-blue flame with a tiny 1/4-inch blue-white cone at the base.

CARBURIZING FLAME
(EXCESS ACETYLENE WITH OXYGEN)

NEUTRAL FLAME

OXIDIZING FLAME
ACETYLENE WITH EXCESS OXYGEN

Grab a mild steel welding rod. It should be about the same diameter as your metal to be welded is thick. Pull your goggles down over your eyes and begin to heat your metal. You can use either a back and forth or a circular motion on the spot to be heated. It should get red hot and start to melt, turning into a puddle. Keep the center cone of the flame inside the puddle area, but keep the tip of the torch from touching the puddle. Now put the end of your rod down in the red hot area and melt them together, then move on. Overheating the metal will cause holes in your work, so don't linger. Keep your torch at a 30° to 45° angle to your work. In most cases you will want the flame pointed in the direction you wish to go. Try to keep a smoothness and continuity to your work.

Once you have finished, shut off the oxygen valve at the torch, then the acetylene torch valve, and then close your cylinder valves. Remember that your metal is still hot, so cool it slowly with water or handle it with pliers or tongs.

Cutting is a slightly different procedure than welding. You will need to put a cutting attachment on your torch. You should set your pressure on the oxygen regulator to 10 lbs., the acetylene remains at

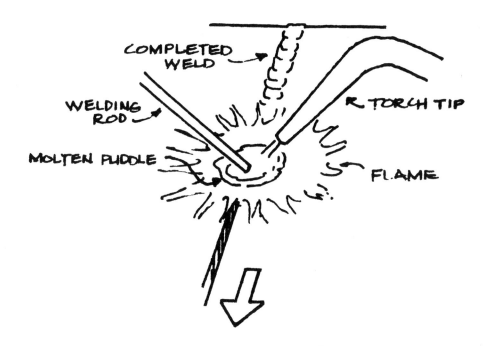

COMPLETED WELD

WELDING ROD

MOLTEN PUDDLE

TORCH TIP

FLAME

about 5 lbs. The oxygen valve on the cutting torch handle (the one right where the hose comes in) should be set completely open during all cutting. The oxy-acetylene mixture is then controlled by the second oxygen valve in the middle of the torch handle.

With a soapstone, mark the place where you intend to cut. Get the flame going as in welding. Tilt the flame slightly in the direction you plan to cut. Hold it over the soapstone mark so that the tiny blue-white flame is just touching it. Now the procedures is to heat up that spot till it is red hot (this will take anywhere from 30 to 60 seconds, depending on the thickness of the metal), and then jolt it with a blast from your oxygen lever, which up to now you haven't used. When it gets red hot (and you may have to pull the flame away every so often to check), squeeze the lever and hold tight. Sparks will spew, the noise will suddenly become ferociously loud, a hole will appear in your metal, and it will seem like you are just about to topple into a volcano. When that hole appears, start moving along your cutting line, with the flame still $1/8$-inch above the surface. If you move too quickly, your cut won't go all the way through. If you move too slowly, the slag behind the flame will drip back into the cut and harden. This is the trickiest part of cutting and it's just a matter of practice till you get the feel of how fast to go. If you've done it right, your metal will just fall apart. Chances are, the first few times you cut you will have gone too slowly somewhere along the way and there will be cooled slag in part of the cut. Usually a whack with a hammer on the offending section will separate it. If not, just go back and cut again.

THE UNIVERSAL STAND

We'd like to be able to give you detailed plans for a stand that is light, sturdy, easy to transport, well-behaved, capable of holding everything from a set of kettledrums to the bells on your toes, and inexpensive to boot. Well, there's just no such device. Actually, the best all-around way to hold instruments so that they produce the finest tone with the least interference from the stand would be either a ten-armed Hindu deity, a trained octopus, or better yet, a bunch of friends. But rarely are these immediately available. So we have tried to come up with several alternatives from which you can choose the most suitable one, depending on the needs of your instrument, the size of your shop, and the cash in your wallet.

BASES

First, a stand needs a solid, level base—something large enough to support more than one instrument at a time, heavy enough to keep from tipping over no matter how frenzied the music, and pleasing to look at. The most basic base is a square piece of wood at least 2 feet wide and at least 1 inch thick.

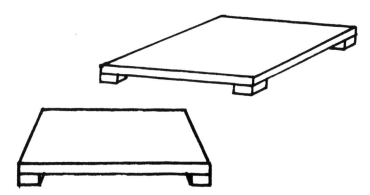

The next step in improving it is to add feet at the corners, so it looks better, and sits more securely. If the feet happen to be something heavier than the wood, say something out of scrap metal bolted on, then the base need not be as wide. Now, if you need an even more stable base and weight is not a consideration, try locating a

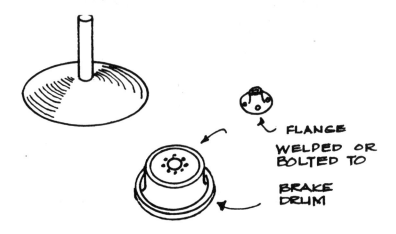

FLANGE
WELDED OR
BOLTED TO

BRAKE
DRUM

plow disc blade, a brake drum, or a wheel hub. These can be bolt-ed or welded onto an upright and will provide more than enough solidity. A floor flange (found in the plumbing section of a hardware store) can be bolted or welded on. Or the metal base can be weld-ed directly to the upright.

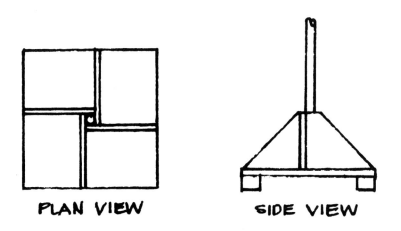

PLAN VIEW   SIDE VIEW

UPRIGHTS

If you are using a wooden base, the simplest upright would be a 1 5/8-inch wooden dowel commonly used in closets to hang clothes from. The dowel can be attached either with a nail (weak), a lag bolt (stronger), or a bracing system (strongest).

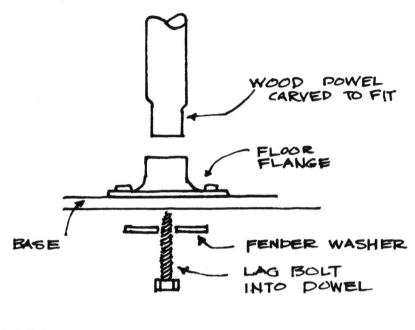

WOOD DOWEL CARVED TO FIT

FLOOR FLANGE

BASE

FENDER WASHER

LAG BOLT INTO DOWEL

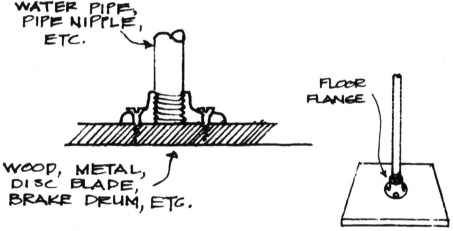

WATER PIPE, PIPE NIPPLE, ETC.

FLOOR FLANGE

WOOD, METAL, DISC BLADE, BRAKE DRUM, ETC.

Or you may wish to bolt a floor flange to the base into which you screw a 6-inch or longer pipe nipple whose inside diameter is large enough to hold your dowel. The next step up in both stability and cost would be to substitute a threaded water pipe for the dowel and screw this directly into the floor flange. Or if you don't want to use threaded pipe, bolt a wooden plug inside some metal tubing and then attach that to your base.

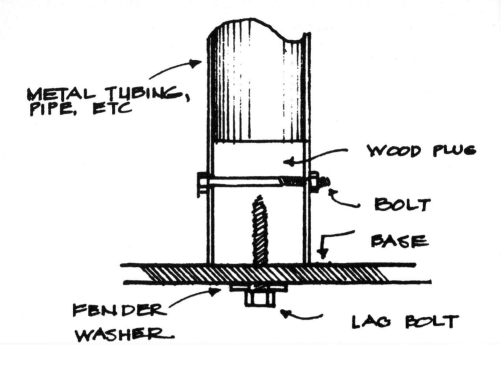

METAL TUBING, PIPE, ETC

WOOD PLUG

BOLT

BASE

FENDER WASHER

LAG BOLT

Welding in many ways is the best option: simple, permanent, and elegant. Most of our stands have plow disc blade bases with a length of exhaust pipe welded onto it. If you choose to use conduit instead of exhaust pipe here is a word of CAUTION: Galvanized water pipe and conduit are coated with zinc. When you heat this metal in the welding process, it releases a poisonous gas. So if you decide to use either of these, exercise all precautions, such as proper ventilation, use of a respirator, etc.

TOPS

If you want a wooden top for your stand, the best way to attach it to the upright is to bolt another floor flange to the underside of the top. If your upright is threaded pipe then you merely screw the pipe directly into the flange. If you are using a wooden dowel or a non-threaded exhaust pipe, then you should screw into the flange a 6-inch nipple whose inside diameter is slightly larger than the diameter of the upright. Of course, if you are welding your stand together, then you can weld on whatever shape metal you wish to complete your top.

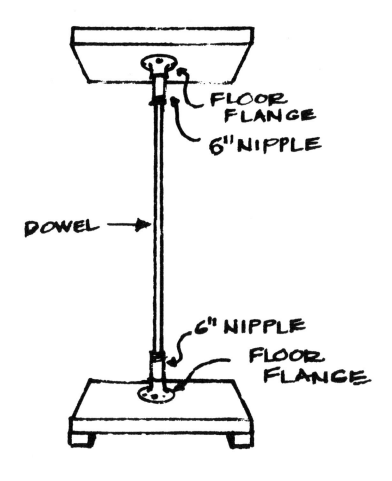

FLOOR FLANGE

6" NIPPLE

DOWEL →

6" NIPPLE

FLOOR FLANGE

The height of stands varies greatly depending on the size of the person who will be using it and whether it is being used to hold flat objects like saw blade bells, or tall ones like artillery shells. So it would be to your advantage to sketch out some plans for your stands first before going out and collecting the necessary materials.

Sound loss through floor absorption may be a problem for some of your instruments, so it is good to have an extra sheet of neoprene available to place under the base of your stand. Sound loss can also occur in the stand itself. So try to ensure that the interface between the instrument and the stand has optimal flexibility built into it. Heavy foam, neoprene, springs, or other suspension systems will allow the instrument to project its sound out into the room rather than be soaked up by the stand.

METAL

AGOGO BELLS

AGOGO BELLS

The origin of this instrument, like so much of our percussion heritage, is found in Africa. From there it came to the Americas, where its greatest use is in providing a fundamental rhythm for samba in Brazil. Agogo bells come in a wide variety of styles, including three-bell versions. The pattern we give here is simple and will do for starters.

From a junkyard or sheet metal supplier, obtain some cold-rolled steel, at least 20 gauge. VW fenders and roofs are approximately the same thickness and may be more available. Or use the metal from an old 55-gallon oil drum. The heavier gauges are a bit harder to work with, but they sound better.

Draw two right angle patterns on your metal sheets:

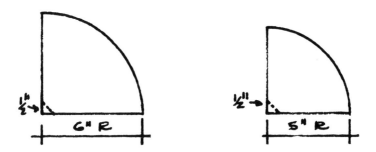

If you prefer a shorter, wider bell, increase the angle. The measurements are approximate. You may want something larger or smaller. But these proportions will produce two notes approximately a third apart.

Cut out the pieces with tin snips, the biggest you can find. This is blister work, so wear gloves. If you can obtain some compound-lever metal cutters they will make your work much easier. Next, cut off a $1/2$-inch triangle from each corner as shown. This will give you a hole at the end of your bell.

Now bend the metal into cone shapes. A good shaping device is two 2x4s and a 2x3 in a vise or nailed together.

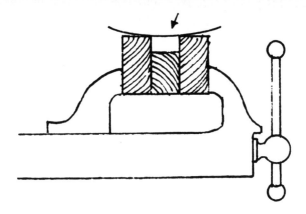

Hammering the metal between the 2x4s starts the curve properly, and you can finish it by working it further on the pointed end of an anvil or a cone-shaped piece of wood or even a baseball bat in a vise. Try to get the two edges as close together as possible.

Now weld the joint together with welding rod. Use a small tip on your torch. After you have welded the seams on your bells, weld them onto a 10 or 12-inch piece of ¼-inch steel welding rod, or similar diameter steel tubing.

Bend the handle to bring the two bells close to each other but not touching. It is easier to bend the handle if it is heated first, but it can also be done cold. Any thin piece of metal rod will work well as a beater. If you wish to raise the pitch of your bells, cut some metal from the edge.

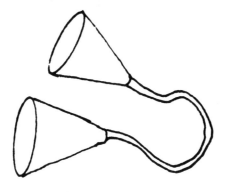

Trim off the excess around the rim of each bell. Heat up the bells red hot with a large tip on your torch, and then plunge them into water. This will harden them and purify the tone.

Two of the traditional agogo bell rhythm patterns from Brazil are as follows: The *Hi* and *Lo* indicate which bell to strike.

COWBELLS

If you have livestock or love Latin American music you may want to make a cowbell. A simple version can be constructed in the following fashion: Take a piece of fender metal or other cold-rolled steel (see the preceding section on agogo bells)—it should be at least 20 gauge, the heavier the better. This is a thickness midway between Volkswagen fenders and 55-gallon drums. The thicker the metal, the richer the tone and the more difficult it is to manufacture. So choose accordingly.

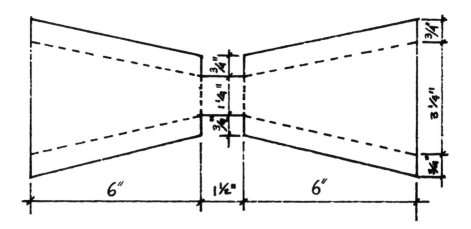

Mark out the above pattern on the metal and cut it with a torch or compound-lever cutters.

Now bend it into shape and weld the seams. Depending on the gauge of the metal, you may need to hammer it a bit to get it into shape.

Your cowbell may be played with a hard wood stick or a large dowel. Latin American cowbell rhythms involve holding the bell in the hand and, with a large dowel, hitting either the lip of the bell or the body. One common rhythm as used in the mambo or cha-cha is the following:

(L = lip of bell, B = base of bell)

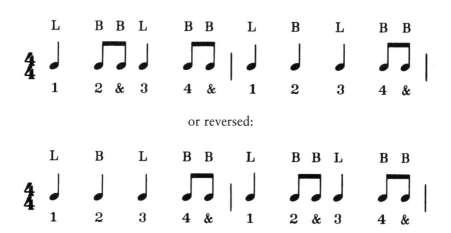

105

BELL CIRCLES

Betty, who took the photos for this book, gave us a set of cowbells from Greece. They are beautifully shaped and have remarkably good tone for pieces of thin steel that are forge welded and riveted together. We left them in a box for some time, unable to decide how they could best be mounted, until we remembered an elderly wheel-barrow that was rusting away out in the boneyard behind the shop. The steel spoke wheel from the wheelbarrow would serve to hold the bells and complement their unusual form.

We took a plow disc blade to which we welded a 7-inch piece of 1^1/$_2$-inch i.d. exhaust pipe. Next, we welded a 3^1/$_2$-inch piece of conduit to the top of a 44-inch long piece of 1^3/$_8$-inch o.d. exhaust pipe. The pipe was then inserted into the conduit, the wheel bolted securely to the top as shown, and the bells wired onto the rim, using the spokes as support. We used 16 gauge mild steel wire, but you might want to try insulated copper wire instead, since the insulation will prevent the wire from rattling about while the instrument is being played.

Now, if you don't have a friend returning from Greece bearing gifts of cowbells, you might try import stores, which often carry an array of inexpensive bells from India. Or you could make your own, using the agogo bell or cowbell patterns found in the preceding sections. Leave a small flange on the rear of the bell so it can be more easily mounted. As for wheels and old hand plows, they often show up at flea markets and junkyards.

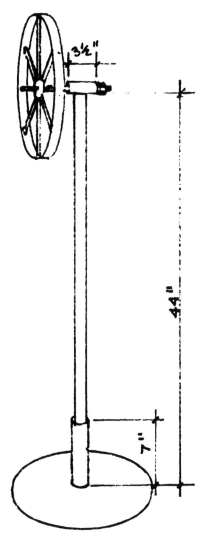

ALUMINUM CLAVES

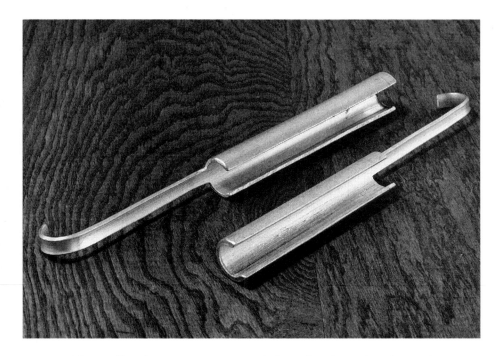

Traditionally, claves are 7 to 9-inch long hardwood rods used to play the most typical of all Latin American rhythms called, naturally enough, clave. It goes like this:

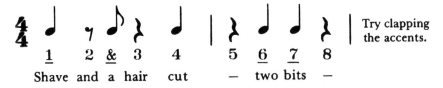

Try clapping the accents.

This rhythm, in either this form or what is known as reverse clave,

is the basis for such typical Latin rhythms as mambo, cha-cha, and pachanga.

You can make claves out of dowels or better yet turn down some hardwood stock on a lathe. But if you don't have a lathe or hardwood, try this version of claves made from ³/₄-inch aluminum pipe (found in a junkyard). They are extraordinarily bright sounding and easy to make. One piece of pipe can yield two claves by marking out the illustrated pattern onto the pipe and then cutting along the lines.

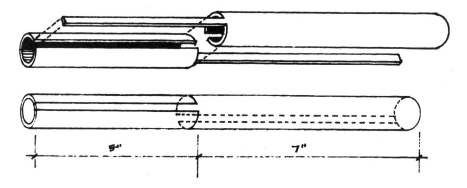

Use a hacksaw or a table or radial arm saw equipped with either a carbide tip blade or an abrasive blade especially designed to cut aluminum. You will be taking a small, light piece of metal and cutting it with a large, heavy, 10,000-toothed shark, so WATCH YOUR FINGERS. For safety, you MUST build a jig to hold the pipe in place while cutting out the handles. Also wear full face and eye protection so that you are not punctured or scratched up by the little chips of aluminum that will be flying about. Oh yes, ear plugs aren't a bad idea, either.

After you have rough cut your clave, file away the burrs with a coarse file and smooth out the sharp edges. You might want to explore altering the tone by cutting a notch in the end furthest from the handle.

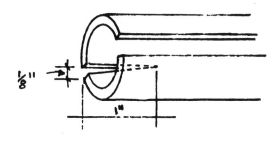

FINGER CYMBALS

Finger cymbals, sometimes called zils, serve as one of the primary musical ingredients of belly dancing. Variations appear in many eastern cultures, where they are used as part of the rhythmic accompaniment for dance. You can fashion your own set of cymbals from the bells found in the older-style telephones. You know the ones: squat, no buttons, basic black. Here's how to do it:

With a torch—either a heating tip on your oxy-acetylene torch, a "Prestolite" torch, a blowtorch, or a Burnsamatic—anneal the bells. Annealing is a process of softening the metal so that it can be worked more easily. If you use a firebrick to work on, heat it first to slow the cooling process even more. Apply your flame to the bells till they are red and glowing. Then let them cool down as slowly as possible.

Once you can handle them, hammer the edges out on a 1-inch or larger nut or a pipe plug, or any large hole with preferably rounded edges. You want to flatten the edges of the bells without making them too thin, or the tone will suffer.

Insert surgical tubing or wide rubber bands into the holes, tie a knot, and slip them over your thumb and forefinger. We buffed ours on a wheel to give them more luster.

A typical belly dance rhythm called *baladi* is:

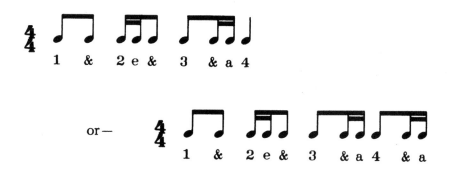

THE ETERNAL TRIANGLE

Next to flea markets and garage sales, the best source of supplies and inspiration for your homemade instruments is a good, sprawling salvage yard. We spent a few hours at one the other day, poking through old cars, scrap metal, and junked machinery, and found aluminum for chimes, disc blades for gongs and bases, universal joint housings for cup gongs, oxygen tanks for big bells, fire extinguisher tanks for small bells, and steel rod for triangles. It's also a good place to find hunks of old chain, if you wish to hang oxygen tank bells. In fact, your imagination is the only limit to the musical instrument materials that can be found there.

The metal you will need for a triangle should be at least $1/2$-inch steel rod. Torsion bars from wrecked cars are made out of top grade metal, though most any steel rod will do. This means, of course, that you are going to end up with one humongous clang machine rather than a delicate orchestral dinger. It will be suitably loud for calling in the hired hands from the fields. And if you don't have hands or fields, you can always kick it or hit it with your head and disturb the peace that way.

Take a 2 to 4-foot piece of rod, and with your torch heat it at two somewhat equidistant places and bend it at 60° angles. An appropriate striker can be made from a 6-inch bolt.

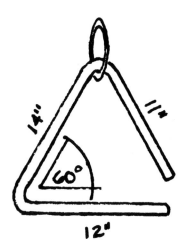

OIL DRUM GONG

GONGS

Gongs belong in that category of "perfect music" described in the section on thumb pianos. With a little restraint, anyone can play them. And with a collection of many gongs in different sizes, shapes, and materials, you can produce rich clouds of sound. Some gongs can be tuned to a specific pitch; others have a non-pitched crash sound like cymbals. And still others can do either depending on where they are struck.

The following section on constructing gongs only touches the surface of a rich musical tradition. But hopefully it will encourage you to explore and experiment further. Listen to the Turkish style cymbals as manufactured by the Zildjian and Paiste companies, to the bells made in Tibet and Nepal, to the glorious gamelans of Indonesia, the tamtams from China and Japan, and more recently the resonated bar gong orchestras being developed by William Colvig and Lou Harrison, Paul Dresher, and Daniel Schmidt, David Doty, and others on the West Coast. All of these are wonderful sources of inspiration and ideas for your investigations and designs.

OIL DRUM GONG

Realizing that the West Indian steel drum orchestras have created some remarkable instruments, we decided to try turning the end of a 55-gallon oil drum into a boss gong. Boss refers to the rounded portion that sticks up in the center of the instrument. This helps give the gong a distinct pitch and as such is useful for tuning.

Select a drum in as healthy a condition as possible. Often you can pick them up for a few dollars from food co-ops that sell safflower and other oils in bulk, or try a paint manufacturer where they use the drums to store linseed oil. If you choose carefully, you may end up with one which has a quart or so of linseed oil on the bottom, and that amount alone will pay for the cost of the drum. Avoid drums which contained paint thinner or other flammables. Cut off the best end—no bungs or dings—with a torch, hacksaw, sawzall, sabre saw, or cold chisel. Leave a 2 to 3-inch rim. This rim will prevent warping of the gong while you are pounding and heating it. The skirt which surrounds it will be removed in the finishing process.

Next, form the boss. For this you will need a mold and a pounding device. Use a large diameter section of pipe or the end of a smallish hi-pressure tank for your mold—anything that has a 4 to 6-inch diameter will do. And for pounding, use a short-handled sledge hammer whose head has been filed to round it more fully, or better yet, a long piece of rod with a rounded weight at one end. With this device you can stand above the gong and easily pound out your boss. Also, don't forget your ear protection. Few of the instruments in this book will give you much satisfaction with impaired hearing. And remember, your neighbors have ears also.

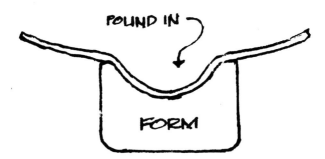

We made our boss 1¹/₂ inches deep and 6 inches wide. Within certain limits, the deeper and wider the boss, the higher the pitch. So choose your own dimensions accordingly.

The next step is to build a roaring bonfire to harden the gong. In Java, they make some gamelan instruments out of steel drums and leave them unfired. But in Trinidad the steel drums are heated, and we found that this produced a clearer tone for this particular shape.

One way to heat treat your gong is to take the remaining portion of your barrel, cut a hole in the side near the bottom, and fill the barrel with wood. Put two pipes across the top to support your gong. In the hole in the side, put a pipe whose other end is attached to a vacuum cleaner that has had its air flow reversed. Make sure it blows rather than sucks or you will quickly destroy both your vacuum and your peace of mind as you watch the fire eat up your pet Hoover.

Lay your gong on top of the pipes. You should place a piece of thin plywood or particle board over the gong to keep the heat from escaping too fast. Keep the flames stoked until the gong is red hot and glowing. At this point pull it off of the fire with a pair of tongs and hose it immediately with cold water.

When your gong is cool enough to handle, you will want to remove the 3 to 4-inch skirt you left on for stability. If you have a grinder, it can be done very easily by grinding through the metal where the barrel top goes over the side. Make sure you remove only the skirt and leave the rim intact.

The last steps are to hammer the metal around the boss to achieve a tightening and reshaping, and to tune it to the desired pitch. For playing use, use a softball bat gonger or other large soft heavy beater, and strike the boss with a firm but light touch for the best tone.

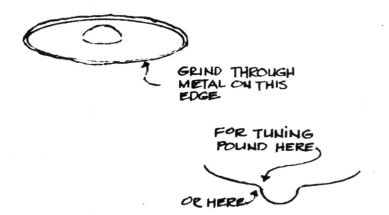

GRIND THROUGH METAL ON THIS EDGE

FOR TUNING POUND HERE

OR HERE

CUP GONGS

Throughout Asia, there are many versions of this lovely instrument. They are often used as part of Buddhist religious ceremonies or in household shrines in Japan. Usually they are made out of brass and either spun or hammered into shape. Cup gongs come in all sizes ranging from 2 inches across the top to 2 feet across. With the price of brass climbing and the many difficulties involved in casting or spinning your own, here are two alternatives.

You know when you drive into a gas station and go over that black wire and you hear DING-DING? Well, that wire is attached to a mechanism that strikes a small bell inside the station. Now, after the gas shortages of 1974 and 1979, many stations have gone out of business and there may still be empty stations on the corners of many urban streets. Presumably, some of those stations still have bells. Find out who owns the property and persuade them to part with that small, unused bell on the wall. They also turn up at flea markets. The bell need only be hung or turned over and placed on a small cushion to be played.

Another automotive source for cup gongs are the universal joint housings from some Chevys vintage 1934 to 1954—the ones with closed drive shafts. They look like this:

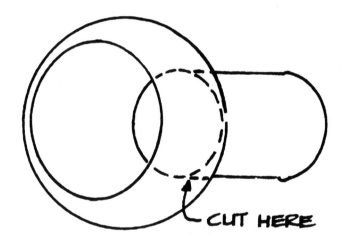

CUT HERE

They are most readily available at junkyards. Once you have removed them from the car, simply take an acetylene torch or hacksaw and cut off the bell part, leaving as much of the bottom intact as possible. Now grind off the rust and glitch with a heavy-duty circular grinder or a belt sander or wire wheel. Three or four of these gongs will give you a nice range of notes. They can be tuned by grinding a small amount off the tops.

DIMPLE GONGS

Rummaging around a metals warehouse in San Jose, we found some plates of aluminum approximately ⅛ inch thick by 12 inches square, as well as several pieces of ⅛-inch aluminum which, how nice, had already been cut into 15-inch diameter circles. We held them and tested their tone. Very promising if a bit unfocused. So we bought them—at $1 a pound the whole bunch came to about $10— and took them home.

At first we considered cutting the plates diagonally and hanging them as triangular chimes, something Mel McBride had done with considerable success. But then in talking with Bill Colvig we learned that we could hammer bosses into them and turn them into pitched gongs. So we tried it, and after a few false starts came up with a set of gongs with lovely tones that were easy to make.

Simply mark the center point on each plate or disc. Place it on the end of a fairly wide piece of soft wood, 4 by 4 inches. Put the round end of a ball-peen hammer on the center mark and smite it hard several times with a small sledge or heavy hammer. A cautionary note: Never take a hammer in each hand and swing them together so that the faces hit. Also, always wear adequate eye protection.

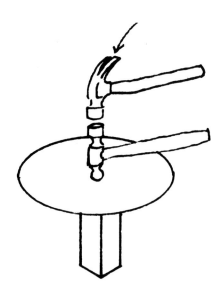

DIMPLE GONGS

The resulting dimple gives the plate not only a distinct pitch, but its name as well–though if you look at it from the other side, it becomes a pimple gong. We found by experimenting that generally, the smaller the dimple the lower the pitch, so tune yours accordingly.

Next, drill holes at the nodal points of the gong to enable you to suspend it properly. The nodes can be found by placing the gong on two pieces of foam so that the surface of the gong is level—you might check this with a level—and so that the dimple is facing up. Sprinkle salt lightly and evenly over the gong, then tap gently with a mallet. The salt will collect at the points of least vibration—the nodes.

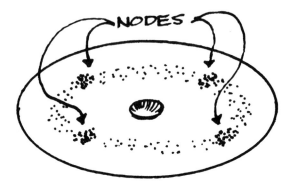

Mark two points several inches apart and drill your holes. On our circular gongs we also drilled a hole in the center of the dimple so that it could be either hung horizontally or mounted on a cymbal stand and struck on the edge. As a final cosmetic touch, you can remove any surface grunge with a circular sander or rotary grinder.

LONG GONGS

The idea for these resonated bars came from the work of William Colvig and Lou Harrison. Bill has built entire sets, tuned carefully to the requirements of the music which Lou composes. We chose to work on a somewhat smaller scale and made two beautifully low-pitched gongs. One is $1/4$ by $6 1/4$ by $23 1/16$ inches with a pitch of G, 98.98 cps. The shorter bar is $1/4$ by $5 3/16$ by $19 3/4$ inches tuned to C, 130.64 cps. Both are aluminum. We suspended them over resonators constructed out of 4-inch diameter ABS pipe—see pages

LONG GONGS

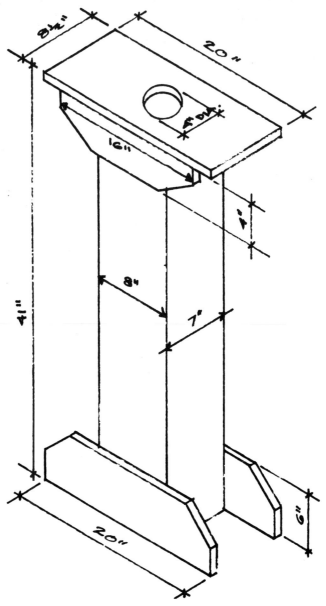

58-60—and suspended the resonators in turn in boxes which we had constructed for another project which, perish the thought, had failed. The G resonator is 33-$\frac{1}{16}$ inches long, the C resonator is 24$\frac{1}{2}$ inches long. Know that the measurements for the bars are subject to the vicissitudes of quality control in the metals industry, and you may end up having an identically sized bar with a different pitch. Your best bet is to start with a longer piece and saw or file off the amount necessary to reach the desired note. This can be checked against a pitch pipe, a tuning fork, or, better yet, a stroboscopic tuner or oscilloscope.

One way of hanging your gongs is to build a rectangular box long enough to house your resonator and at least 3 inches wider than your bar. At the base of the box are supporting feet as shown. Attach to the top of the box a wooden cover whose length is about the same as the bar which it will support. This cover should have a hole in it to accommodate the ABS resonator. (Diagram at left.)

Find the nodes of your bar by taking 22.5% of the total length and marking that distance off from each end. Next mark the nodal points on the cover of your resonator box, and there drill $1/4$-inch diameter holes an inch away from the sides of where the ball will be. Drill holes in the center of four $1\,1/8$-inch diameter dowels each 3 inches long. Attach these to the cover with $1/4$-inch diameter by 5-inch eyebolts as shown.

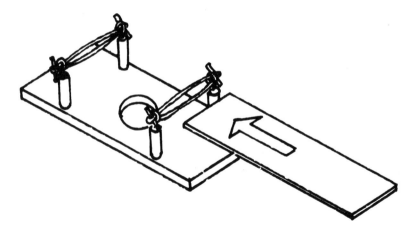

Cut some surgical tubing to a length slightly less than twice the distance between the two eyebolts and tie the ends of the tubing together with wire. Stretch this between the eyebolts using 2-inch sections of $1/4$-inch dowels as restrainers. Slide your bar between the surgical tubing and strike it with a large, heavy mallet with a soft covering. In a pinch your fist will work adequately as a mallet on the larger gongs.

GONG STAND

This stand is a relatively lightweight solution to the problem of hanging your gongs and bells. It does require welding skills and equipment, but apart from that it is a fairly simple project. You will need four pieces of 1½-inch o.d. by 6-foot long exhaust pipe available at auto supply stores. Weld them together in this shape:

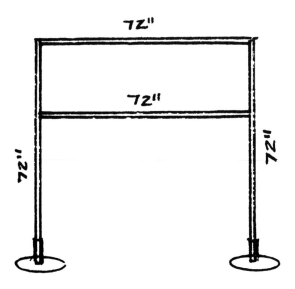

The bases are plow disc blades with 1½-inch i.d. conduit welded on as uprights into which the legs of the stand fit. We drilled

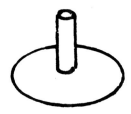

holes in the legs of the pipe and welded on nuts to permit bolts to be used as set screws to keep the stand from bouncing about when you bong your gongs. You might instead wish to drill all the way through both the conduit and exhaust pipe and bolt them in place.

If you are not equipped to make a welded stand, you might consider fashioning one out of wood, or you can make a stand out of threaded water pipe. This will cost more, but it will be sturdy and it can be broken down for transportation purposes—a definite plus.

We recommend ³/₄-inch diameter pipe unless your gongs are particularly light or particularly heavy, which would mean using either ¹/₂ or 1-inch pipe. Here's what you will need for a fairly large stand. Change the measurements to suit your needs.

- 4 — pipe caps
- 6 — 90° ells
- 4 — tees, 2 — unions, 2 close nipples
- 4 — 6-inch nipples
- 4 — 12-inch nipples
- 2 — 42-inch pipe
- 2 — 72-inch pipe
- 2 — 24 inch pipe

These parts are somewhat costly so you might first try scavenging them, or check at your local junkyard. Put it all together in this fashion, using pipe joint compound or a little household oil at the joints, so that you can take it apart if need be.

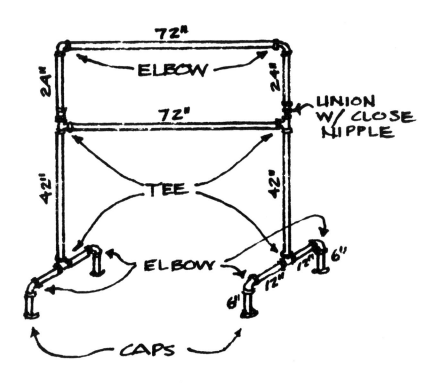

ARTILLERY SHELL BELLS

These bells are ready-built. All you need do is locate them, make sure they have been disarmed so as not to disarm yourself, hit them with a medium-soft mallet, and you will be rewarded with a rich, sustained sound. Over a period of several years, we collected an assortment of shells at the flea market, spending from $2 to $4 for each, though these prices have probably gone up. Half of the shells were brass, the other half steel which had been painted over with a brass-colored protective coating. Using an orbital sander, we cleaned off the glitch and tarnish on the brass shells. Wear a respirator to do this, since little particles of brass float up in the sanding process and are hard on the lungs, not to mention what they make your nose feel like. The steel shells we left as they were. Some of the shells had identical tones, so we cut them to different lengths in order to have a full range of pitches. These shells can be played sitting on their bases. And if you place them on a drum for additional resonance, their tone will be even louder. But played in this manner they may topple over if struck with too much enthusiasm. You can drill a hole in the bottom and suspend them upside down from a wire. Or they can be attached to a stand.

We took a bundle of six $1/2$-inch diameter mild steel rods and jammed them into a piece of pipe attached to a plow disc base and then welded them in place. The rods were then bent backwards and up, and $3/8$ by 1 by 7-inch steel plates were welded onto the end of each rod. Holes had been drilled into each plate, and the shells were bolted on.

A word of CAUTION. None of the shells we found were armed. It is unlikely that any of them would get out of military hands with the primer cap still active. But TAKE ALL NECESSARY PRECAUTIONS. If the base shows signs of detonation, or the shell has had its primer removed, then there is probably no problem. We found several shells which still had a primer rod, so we threw them on a bonfire, hid behind the shop and waited for the 4th of July. Nothing happened, so we assumed that the primer explosive had been removed. But if you have any doubts at all, check first with an explosives expert.

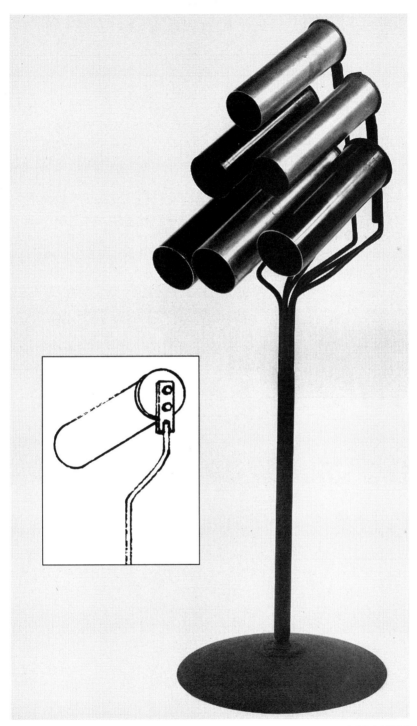

ARTILLERY SHELL BELLS

BELL TREE

Like the artillery shells, the bells for this instrument had accumulated over a period of years. They were usually found at the flea market for a dollar or less—and most of them were at one time used as fire alarm bells situated in stairwells in public buildings and apartment houses. They all have excellent tone since they were specifically designed to be bells. And while they are easily hung from a cord and played that way, we ended up with so many bells that they would have taken up an entire stand if we'd suspended them individually. So instead we devised the following bell tree.

Buy a 3-foot length of ready-bolt, a continuously threaded metal rod that comes in different sizes. The diameter you select will depend on the sizes and types of bells you want to mount. We used a $^3/_8$-inch size for our alarm bells and had to enlarge some of their holes to make them fit. A plow disc blade will make a fine base, though anything heavy will do (a 50-lb bagel?). If you use a disc blade, two large fender washers can be used to cover the hole in the center.

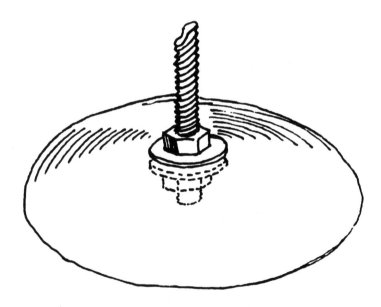

Attach your ready-bolt to the base and then start adding in this order: nut, washer, bell, washer, nut—nut, washer, bell, washer, nut, etc., going from the largest bell to the smallest. This is tedious work, particularly if you plan to use the full length of ready-bolt, which will hold up to fifteen bells. If your collection is smaller, plan ahead and cut the bolt to the length needed, saving yourself what may seem like endless hours twisting on reluctant nuts.

After the first bell is in place, you can speed up the process a bit by putting a little oil on the threads and then screwing on two nuts at a time. Space the gongs to your liking.

If you decide to paint them or refinish them in any way, do it before you put them on the tree.

We threaded a handle on the top of our bolt so that it could be carried and hung more easily.

In the photo on page 130, the bell tree is sitting on a Japanese-style zafu cushion made by Ron Taylor. The tone of the cushion could best be described as somewhat restrained, even distant.

WHEELS OF TIME

Circular saw blades from table saws, radial arm saws, skilsaws, etc., are another good source of bells and have the potential for a unique sound. However, some of the problems in using the blades are how to mount them so that they are playable, how to reinforce the sound so that it is more audible, and how to keep your fingers from being torn to shreds on the sharp edges. Many of the blades when struck emphasize only the higher harmonics. To correct this we discovered that when the blades are held near a flat surface—about $1/4$ to $1/2$-inch away, the sound is stronger and deeper. So we decided to mount the blades close to each other, and we produced an exotic and dangerous looking instrument that we have called the Wheels of Time—a title that barely won out over Jaws.

Blades may be acquired cheaply on the ubiquitous flea market/garage sale circuit or from lumberyards and cabinet shops or saw sharpening places where they are discarded when they warp or their teeth break.

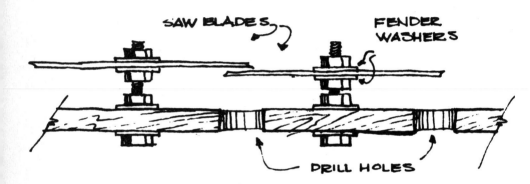

For a base we used a discarded slit-drum bottom with holes drilled in the top. Most any box open on the bottom will do, depending on how many saw blades you wish to support. Bolt $1/4$ by $1^1/4$-inch bolts into the top of the box as shown. Then add a second nut, a $1^1/4$-inch fender washer over the nut, next the blade, another washer, and finally the top nut. Small rubber washers, inserted between blades and the fender washers, may be useful in preventing unwanted tones.

The rear row of blades can be positioned a little above and over the front row as shown in the photograph. This can be done by raising your second nut a little higher. Try to make the space between the blades as close as possible but not to the point where they touch when you strike the outer edges with any force. Another effective arrangement is shown in the drawing at right:

134

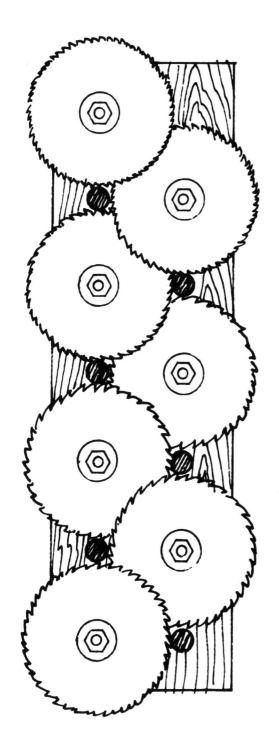

The finished
instrument can
be played with a
variety of mal-
lets for a full
range of sound.

OXYGEN TANK BELLS

Superb quality bells can be made from the high-pressure cylinders used to hold oxygen, helium, nitrous oxide, and other gaseous delights. This is yet another of Lou Harrison and Bill Colvig's imaginative ideas on how to recycle ordinary industrial materials.

Tanks can be bought occasionally at the flea market. Try not to pay more than $20 for the larger tanks. Perhaps an even better source of supply is your local industrial gas distributor and of course your friendly scrap metal yard. All high-pressure tanks must be periodically checked for defects. Any rejects are stamped as such and can no longer be used to store gas. So they are usually sold as scrap, and you may find a dealer willing to part with his rejects at low cost. They come in all sizes from just inches to 5 feet long and sometimes even longer. And they all make lovely bells.

It is possible to cut these tanks (particularly the smaller ones) with a hacksaw, or an abrasive blade on your skilsaw. But the big ones will eat up a few blades in the process, and a lot of your time and calories. It's so much easier to cut them with an oxy-acetylene torch that it would be worth your while to rent a unit for this particular instrument. Or use a friend's.

If you go the rental route, first get all your tanks together, prepare your work space, and mark with soapstone the places where you intend to cut your tanks. The rental places charge you for time, and the more you can do in advance before you rent the equipment, the less moola you end up paying. You will also need a large vehicle to carry the equipment—a van, station wagon, or pickup. For cutting procedures see the section on welding.

When you finish you will have twice as many bells as you had tanks to start with. Before you put your equipment away, test the bells for pitch—providing you can hold them off of the floor long enough to give them a whack with a hammer or mallet and not end up with a hernia for your efforts. You may find that some of them have the same pitch and need more cutting to vary the tuning. The torch cut edges can then be ground off with a portable grinder enhancing both the appearance and tone.

OXYGEN TANK BELLS

The next problem is how to hang the bells, and for this we offer two solutions: the quick-and-easy-and-a-bit-funky version, or the classy model.

Before you return your torch, cut a hole through the bottom of the lower half of each tank. Use your big tip for the job and make sure the hole is wide enough to admit a $1/2$-inch bolt. Next, take a hammer or blunt screwdriver and clean off the slag around the rim of each bell. For the shorter bell (presuming it's less than arm's length), take a $1/2$-inch diameter bolt with two nuts and a washer and attach as indicated in the drawing.

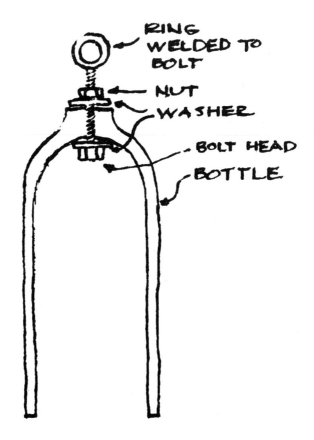

On the longer bell—if it's over arm's length—you can put the tank in an inverted position on some convenient holder like say your toilet and try dropping bolts down the tank, hoping that one will somehow land tip first in the hole. But your tank may partially rust away before you succeed, so it is suggested that you try the East Aptos Wire Trick, which is: Lay the tank on its side. Take a long, relatively inflexible length of wire and thread it through the hole, pushing it until it appears at the rim. Now stick it through a washer and wrap it around the bolt (the bolt should be $1/2$ by 5 inches or longer, the washer at least $1^1/2$ inches in diameter). Then draw this back up through the hole, attach two nuts and two washers as indicated and, voilà! your handle. Hang with durable wire or rope from any strong support and strike it with a heavy wooden dowel, a ball bat bonger, or scavenged piano leg. The tone is richest closest to the rim. It's also loud and carries well, so save your pealing of bells, and orgies of sound till the daytime when the neighbors are at work.

The more elegant solution to the hanging problem is to find a

hardware store well equipped enough to carry 5-inch long eyebolts, with $1/2$ to $5/8$-inch thread on the shaft. Should there be none in your town, you can fashion them in the following manner: With your torch, heat $3/8$-inch steel rod until it is hot enough to bend around a pipe 1 to 2 inches in diameter. Then weld that ring onto a bolt with a washer at the head end. Make sure, on any bell longer than arm's length, that you have drawn the bolt through the hole before you weld on the ring.

If you have opted for the elegant approach you may want something more pleasing to the eye than the chipped and rusted paint job that covers the outside of most tanks we've seen. You can either paint over it (the paint won't appreciably alter the tone), or you can sand it off and then give it several coats of lacquer. This leaves a beautifully naturally silvery-metallic finish. Be warned that this involves a lot of work and if you do it on only one bell, it will seriously outclass all the others. You can strip the paint with strip-ease and sand it by hand. Using a belt sander would be possible but difficult. It would be better to use a disc grinder with a rough grit #16 disc for the job. You may need several discs if you've cut more than one tank. They clog up with paint fairly quickly. For smaller tanks (nitrous oxide size) a vise is nice for holding the tank while you work. Wear goggles and a respirator. Don't forget your eye and ear protection. When you've finished sanding, clean off the dust and residue, then cover the tank with a coat of lacquer.

Unless you have an unusually large house or studio, or have made all your bells on the short side, you will probably want to hang them outside. A really stout tree limb over 5 inches in diameter will bear the weight of several of the larger bells. The tree would most assuredly appreciate being protected by using a canvas collar stuffed with kapok surrounding the rope at the place where it goes around the limb. Another good place to hang your bells is under the eaves of your garage, studio, or house.

SKIN

TUBE DRUMS

TUBE DRUMS

Tube drums are relatively easy instruments to construct, and the resulting sound is nice and robust. What you will need is several pieces of thick-walled cardboard tubing. You can find these as heavy-duty mailing tubes, cores for rolled linoleum and carpeting, or molds for concrete forms. Check your bookstore, furniture store, or construction supply store. We even found some very sturdy tubes for sale in a fabric store. They were being sold as inexpensive bases for outdoor tables. The diameter of the tube can be anywhere between 3 and 12 inches though we've found that something between 6 and 10 inches generally works best. The wall of the tube should be at least $1/4$-inch thick.

Cut your tubing with the longest section being no greater than 36 inches. The rest of your tubes can each be $3/4$ of the length of the preceding one. This is an arbitrary figure but it will give a fairly even distribution of tones. For fine tuning you can saw more off the end of the tube to raise the pitch. Once the pitch is raised it can't be lowered, so be cautious with your saw. If you are not interested in a specific tuning try the following lengths: $34^{1}/_{2}$ inches, $27^{1}/_{2}$ inches, $20^{1}/_{2}$ inches, $15^{1}/_{2}$ inches, $11^{1}/_{2}$ inches.

The next step is mostly cosmetic, so if sound, not looks, is your main objective, skip this paragraph. We painted our drums to make them look a little spiffier and to cut down on the possibility that moisture would hurt the cardboard. Seal them inside and out, and the ends as well, with two coats of an enamel paint.

While your tubes are drying, the next step is to go soak your heads, the drum heads of course—nothing personal. The kind of heads needed are a thin goat skin available at larger music stores or by mail from United Rawhide Mfg. Inc., 1644 No. Ada St., Chicago, IL 60622. Specify the 10-inch size if your tubes are no larger than 7 inches in diameter. You will need at least $1^{1}/_{2}$-inch overlap.

After your heads have soaked in warm water for about an hour—the thicker the skin, the longer they should be soaked—take them out of the water and wipe off the excess moisture. Do not attempt to dry them. They should be wet but not dripping. What

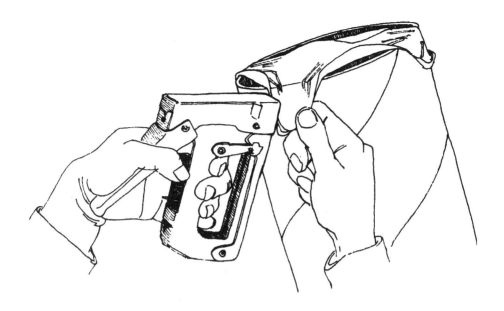

you will need is a pair of vise grips or pliers, a staple gun, and a friend.

Place the wet skin over the opening and staple one side. Now, with one of you holding the vise grips, pull down the other side as *tightly as you can* without tearing the skin. Next, do the quarter sections as in the diagram and work your way around the drum in this fashion. When you have the first eight staples in you can fill in the rest without having to keep stapling diametrically. Be sure to keep stretching as you staple. Put your staples about as far apart as the staples are wide. Make your final round of staples at an angle to the rest to prevent slippage of the skin when it dries. Most importantly, make sure that you have pulled the skin TIGHT. This involves a fair amount of elbow grease but it pays off on foggy days or during the rainy season, because the skin will surely soften, and if the head is not tight enough, the tone will disappear. This can be corrected temporarily by holding the drum near a lamp or spotlight.

After you have finished stapling, trim off the excess skin and, if you wish to cover up the staples, wrap the rim with tape. Use masking tape to hold the wet skin in place while it is drying. When dry, replace that with duct tape or any of the 3M colored vinyl tapes.

For a stand, drill ¼-inch diameter holes through each drum 3 inches from the top. Next, put threads on both ends of a 3-foot length of ¼-inch diameter welding rod. There is a little device called a threading die which will thread your rod for you. If you don't have a threading die, use a length of ready-bolt or all-thread. Now take two pairs of 38-inch long, lightweight steel tubing and braze or weld on a fender washer to each pair as shown. The rod is then inserted through the tube drums and bolted to the legs. A simpler version can be built by substituting a dowel for the welding rod and wooden 1x2s for the metal legs. A triangular wooden plate can replace the fender washer.

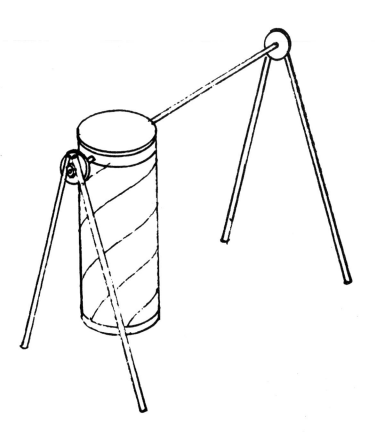

BALIMBAFON

We were in Los Angeles a few years ago and were poking around the more interesting back corners of Drum City—actually all the corners of this unique store are interesting—when we noticed an unusual set of drums called boo bams. They had individual resonators and were tuned chromatically. We inquired at the counter if we might take some measurements of the drums, only to be rebuffed by a salesperson who probably had inhaled more than his share of freeway smog on the way to work that day.

But as we prepared to leave, another man, who had apparently overheard our conversation, mentioned to us that if we came back after hours he would let us in to take whatever measurements we needed. It turned out that the man was Roy Harte, one of the owners of the store, an author of several percussion books, a collaborator at different times with Harry Partch, and obviously someone sympathetic to the needs of other instrument builders.

We left L.A. with our measurements and a copy of one of the resonators, but the project remained untouched for some time. There was some fairly complex machine work involved with constructing the tensioning devices. We tried making a prototype out of irrigation pipe and aluminum couplings, but the amount of work involved hardly made a whole set of these drums worth our time until we began using ABS pipe for resonators. Then it occurred to us that we could make the tensioning devices out of plastic also. Lucite seemed the best choice since it is strong, comes in all thicknesses, and is beautiful in its own fashion. So we bought some and found that the price of beauty can be steep. But we decided that the expense was worth it if the material did the job properly. Well, there is one quality of Lucite which we didn't know about. It's extremely brittle and doesn't like being assaulted with blades or drill bits unless one takes extra precautions. We had several shattering failures until we realized that to drill it successfully, one must use pilot holes and drill from both sides of the piece to avoid splitting the material.

As it turned out, we could have used ³/₄-inch plywood or ¹/₄-inch aluminum instead. So unless you have a particular fondness for Lucite and are equipped to deal with it properly, try either of the other materials. Here's how to proceed. You will need a 20-foot section of 4-inch diameter ABS pipe and four 4-inch diameter couplings cut in half. Cut the pipe to the following lengths.

33 ⁷/₁₆"	21 ⁷/₈"
29 ⁵/₈"	19 ³/₈"
26 ⁵/₁₆"	18 ¹/₄"
24 ³/₄"	16 ¹/₈"

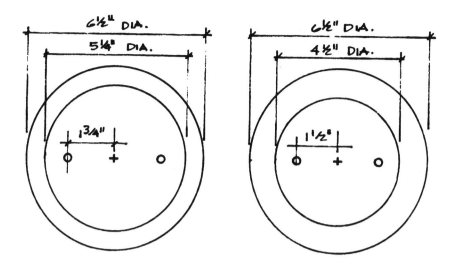

Next, take a 2 by 5-foot sheet of $^3/_4$-inch plywood or $^1/_4$-inch aluminum. Cut out eight circles with a 6$^1/_2$-inch o.d. and a 5 $^1/_4$-inch i.d. for the tops and eight circles with a 6$^1/_2$-inch o.d. and 4 $^1/_2$-inch i.d. for the bottoms. You might want to use aluminum for the top rings and plywood for the bottom ones. The easiest way to do this is to use a circle cutter in a drill press. General Hardware makes a model No. 55 for a $^1/_2$-inch chuck which is ideal. Draw your circles. Then mark two spots approximately one sixth of the diameter from the edge of the finished inside disc and diagonally opposite each other. Bolt your material down at these spots to the drill press table. Cut the outside circle with the point of the cutter facing out. Face the point in when you cut the inside circle. Run the circle cutter at slow speeds only. Keep your hands away while the cutter is spinning. If you are using aluminum you will be left with your circle and, as a bonus, a small disc with two holes at the nodes which can be hung as a mini gong.

If you don't have access to a drill press use a bandsaw for the outside diameter and a sabre saw to cut out the middle. Or do it all with a sabre saw and a coping saw. It will be a tedious operation but it will work.

Now you will need to fashion eight hold-down rings out of $^1/_8$-inch diameter welding rod—at the welding supply place they may refer to it as filler metal or filler steel or gas rod. Shape the rings by

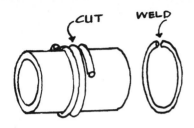

CUT   WELD

bending the rod around your ABS pipe, and then weld or solder them together. If this operation is too much for the capabilities of your shop, take the rings to a machine shop or welding shop and they will do it up for you in a flash.

Next, you will need to drill eight equally spaced holes in each of the circles. Separate them into pairs of one large and one small ring. Use a ⅛-inch bit and drill through a pair at a time making sure you mark which holes line up together.

Now take four ABS 4-inch couplings, cut them in half and glue them onto one end of each section of the tube. Slide up the smaller i.d. ring under the coupling and glue it in place.

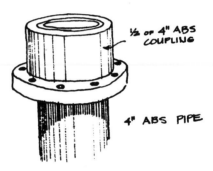

½ of 4" ABS COUPLING

4" ABS PIPE

Soak eight 9-inch diameter heads—see appendix for availability—for an hour or so. The next part requires four hands so borrow a friend. You will be fitting the hold-down ring over the head as you tuck the head inside the top circle. Use vise grips to pull up the flap evenly all around while your friend holds the circle tight. Now put in your bolts—3-inch 10-24 flat head machine screws—and fasten them down to nuts underneath the lower circle. Make sure that as you tighten down you keep the tension somewhat even. The upper circle should end up at least flush with the top of the head. Doing the initial snugging of the heads while the heads are still slightly damp is okay, but let them dry thoroughly before the final tightening and tuning. Also, don't cut off the excess skin until you've declared victory. Tune the drums to a diatonic scale starting with G an octave and a half below middle C.

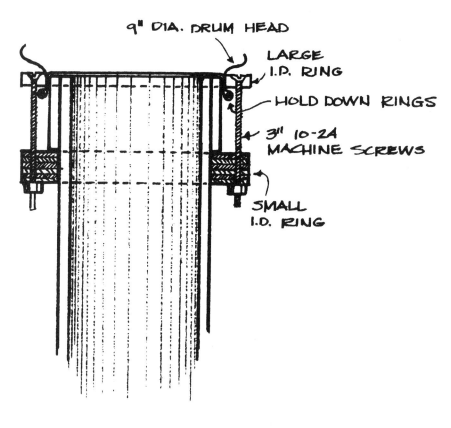

9" DIA. DRUM HEAD

LARGE
I.D. RING

HOLD DOWN RINGS

3" 10-24
MACHINE SCREWS

SMALL
I.D. RING

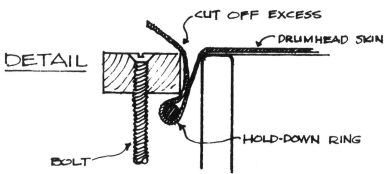

CUT OFF EXCESS

DRUMHEAD SKIN

DETAIL

HOLD-DOWN RING

BOLT

Your stand can be similar in design to the marimba stands, pages 63-66. However, you should use ½- to ¾-inch plywood for the top for greater stability. The front legs are 37 inches long and are tilted forward 15°. The rear legs are 35 inches long and are vertical.

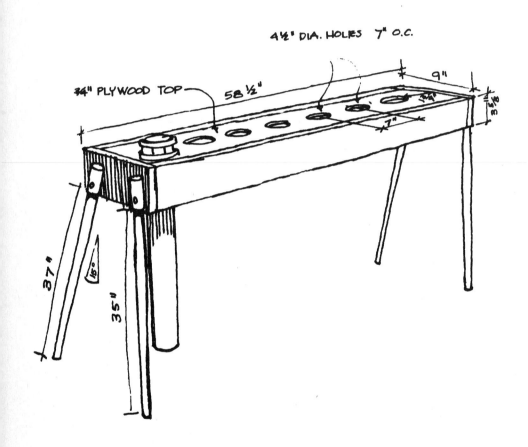

CUICA

The cuica (*kwee*-ka) is a friction drum used in much of Brazil's samba music. It makes a strange assortment of sounds ranging from human cries to dogs barking to a deep roar depending on the size and materials of the drum and the playing techniques involved.

One way to make a cuica is as follows: Take a 10 to 14-inch long section of heavy-duty cardboard tubing such as the type used to make the tube drums in this section. It should be at least 7 inches in diameter. Prepare a 12 to 16-inch length of ¹/₄-inch dowel by planing it down a bit to make it more flexible. Soak a drum head which is at least 3 inches larger than the diameter of your tube. After an hour or so, remove the head from water, and while it is still wet place the dowel in the center and wrap thin wire tightly around the head $\frac{1}{8}$-inch from the end of the dowel.

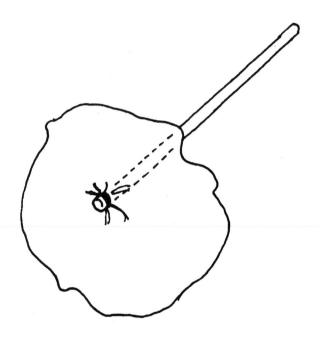

Next staple the head to the tube in the manner described for tube drums. Let it dry before pulling on the stick or you will have to start over.

Playing the drum involves rubbing the stick with the finger and thumb of one hand while holding the drum in the other arm and adjusting the tension of the head by placing the free hand on the skin and alternately pressing and releasing. The rubbing must create enough friction on the stick to cause it to vibrate. This can best be done by moistening the fingers, or hold the stick with a small, damp piece of cloth, moistened with water or a mix of deodorized kerosine and powdered rosin. Or, coat the stick with beeswax, sold at hardware stores as a means of putting a non-skid finish on the handles of carpenters' hammers.

PLASTIC

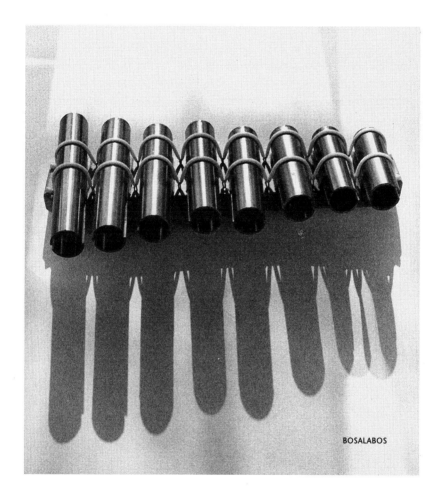

BOSALABOS

BOSALABOS

Once we started using ABS pipe for resonators and tube drums, many new instrument possibilities opened up. But we have had a real love-hate relationship with this remarkable material. ABS chips are now in every corner of the shop. There is a distinctly chemical smell to deal with when one cuts the stuff. It needs fairly toxic solvents to be glued properly, and it is an oil by-product and therefore not a renewable resource like wood. Nor does it have the warmth and friendliness of wood. But it does have many applications and surprisingly good musical tone in its own right.

At Mel McBride's suggestion we tried making a slit drum by capping both ends of a 2-foot section of 4-inch diameter ABS, and then cutting two tongues into it. The resulting sound was excellent. But cutting it was a very dicey operation. The sabre saw melted the plastic as it tried to cut it and the whole process kept bogging down in a sea of black goop. What we ended up with looked like it had once been part of a guard rail on an L.A. freeway. But in spite of this it sounded good.

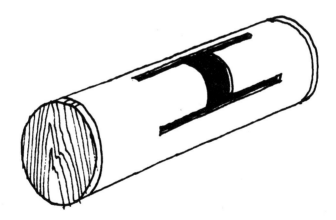

In the meantime, however, we realized that the ABS would be perfect for end-tongued drums like the square boos (see page 19). So we took some 2-inch diameter ABS and cut it to the following lengths:

Note	Drum Length	Length of Slot	Note	Drum Length	Length of Slot
C	15"	$4^5/_{16}$"	G	$10^3/_8$"	$3^1/_4$"
D	$13^5/_8$"	$3^7/_8$"	A	$9^3/_{16}$"	$2^7/_8$"
E	$11^{13}/_{16}$"	$3^9/_{16}$"	B	$8^1/_8$"	$2^9/_{16}$"
F	$11^1/_8$"	$3^7/_{16}$"	C	$7^{11}/_{16}$"	$2^3/_8$"

We glued on plywood discs to cover the unslotted end of the tubes, and called the finished product a bosalabo.

To make a stand, glue two strips of foam to some wood as shown. Staple loops of surgical tubing in two rows the width of the stand. The tubing should be tight enough to hold the tubes in place yet not crush the foam. Slide the bosalabos under the tubing and bolt it to a universal stand. We have also used 3 and 4-inch diameter bosalabos with excellent results. Superball mallets are perfect for this instrument. The tone is both rich and buoyant.

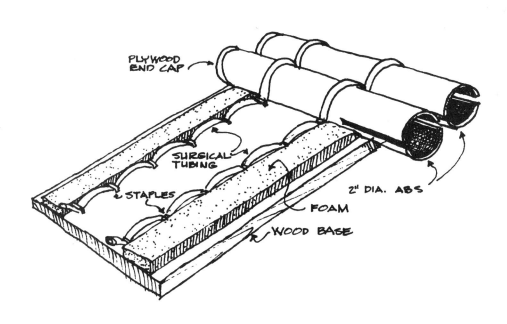

STAMPING TUBES

Stamping tubes appear in many of the musical cultures of the world. Their beauty lies in the ease with which they can be built and played, and the fact that they can be played simultaneously by so many people.

Any durable tubing will do for your stampers, but bamboo or 2-inch diameter ABS pipe work well. Cut the tubes to varying lengths—for example:

68"	54 1/4"	45 5/8"	38 1/4"
61"	51 1/4"	40 1/2"	34"

If you are fortunate enough to have a supply of large (1 to 3-inch) bamboo, you will need to remove the pith on the inside at each node, leaving the bottom one intact. A red hot poker will do the trick. If, however, you are using ABS pipe, you should seal the bottom with a disc of 1/4-inch plywood. Glue the disc on with ABS cement.

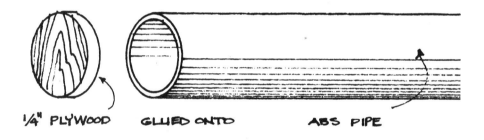

1/4" PLYWOOD   GLUED ONTO   ABS PIPE

To play stamping tubes, simply strike the bottom on the ground. Experiment with playing on different surfaces. We tried ours on a dense neoprene mat and the sound was excellent. Hard packed earth or concrete pavement are also good, though the pavement will eventually eat away the bottoms of your tubes. But it's no problem to glue on replacements. A variation you might try is to put a handful of small rocks in your stamping tube, and a variation on that variation is to glue both ends with rocks inside for a stereophonic rattle. By all means make variations. Write us a letter and tell us what you come up with.

RED DEVILS

Here is yet another way of making temple blocks. These don't sound quite as harmonically rich as wooden ones, but the tone is bright and the instrument is easy to build. We painted ours a rakish red with black tops and thus they acquired their name.

With your leftover scraps of 4-inch ABS pipe from any of the other projects collect seven pieces and cut to these lengths:

4 1/2"	4"	3 1/2"	3"
4 1/4"	3 3/4"	3 1/4"	

At a plastics outlet or larger hardware store pick up some 1/8-inch Lucite for your tops. A 1 by 2-foot piece should be sufficient. Plywood will also work if Lucite is unavailable. On a band saw, sabre saw, or with a coping saw cut out seven circles 4 1/2 inches in diameter. Also cut out seven circles of plywood the same size for the bottoms. For this use a circle cutter on a drill press if you have one, otherwise the band saw, sabre saw, or coping saw will do. Next, drill a hole in the center of each plywood disc and pound in a tee nut. Glue the tops and bottoms onto the ABS sections. Make sure the tee nut is on the inside of the bottom piece before gluing.

Now cut 3/8-inch wide slots in your sections (see diagram on next page):

Size of Section	Distance of Slot from Top
4 1/2"	1/2"
4 1/4"	5/8"
4"	3/4"
3 3/4"	3/4"
3 1/2"	15/16"
3 1/4"	1"
3"	1 1/8"

If you are using a radial arm saw to cut the slots, raise it up 3/4-inch above the table so that it only cuts part way into the section. This may be tricky, so consider clamping a jig to the saw table to help you hold the ABS in place. Always be very careful, and WATCH YOUR FINGERS. If you are not trying to use up leftover ABS, it might be easier in the long run to purchase a 5-foot section

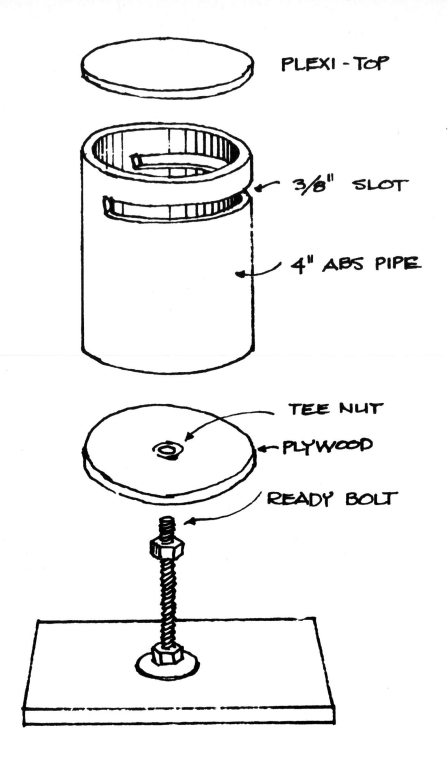

PLEXI-TOP

3/8" SLOT

4" ABS PIPE

TEE NUT

PLYWOOD

READY BOLT

of ABS pipe and cut the slots first before cutting it into sections. This will give you more to hold onto, though you will still want to elevate the fence on your saw table to keep the pipe more secure while you are cutting.

If you are using a handsaw, you will need to nail two pieces of scrap 3/4-inch wood to a table for a jig—see illustration. Then saw down to, but not into, the jig which will give you the correct depth for the slot.

After all the slots have been cut, and tops and bottoms glued on, and instruments painted, if that is your choice, you can make a stand by drilling seven holes into a piece of wood or metal and inserting 1/4 to 5/16-inch readybolt depending on the size of the tee nuts in your red devils. Tighten this down with washers and nuts on either side of the stand, attach a lock nut and screw into the tee nut. This small stand can now be attached to a universal stand.

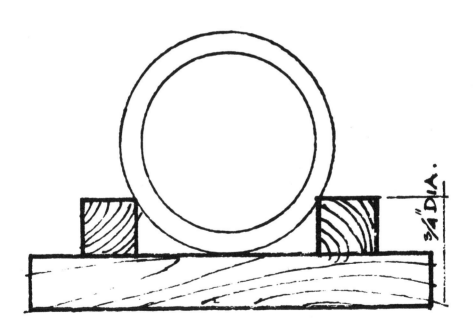

KYDEX DRUMS

If you don't have the time or the tools to construct the tunable ABS balimbafon described on pages 145-150, you might want to try these. They are not as loud or as versatile, but you can build them quickly and cheaply, and the tone is remarkably good for an all-plastic drum.

From a plastics outlet buy a 1 by 2-foot sheet of kydex—a trade name for a very durable, resilient vinyl. It is flexible enough to be twisted and bent without cracking and it serves quite nicely as a synthetic drum head. Unlike skin, it is permanent—a definite plus if the drums are to be used by children.

Cut eight lengths of 4-inch ABS pipe:

33 $\frac{1}{2}$"	21 $\frac{7}{8}$"
29 $\frac{3}{4}$"	19 $\frac{1}{2}$"
26 $\frac{3}{8}$"	18 $\frac{1}{4}$"
24 $\frac{3}{4}$"	15 $\frac{7}{8}$"

Glue onto one end of each length a 4-inch diameter ABS coupling that has been cut in half. Using one of the couplings for a pattern, draw out eight circles on the kydex. Cut these out with heavy scissors or tin snips, then glue them to the couplings, which you will then glue to the tubes using ABS cement. The drums can now be mounted in the same stand used for the balimbafon.

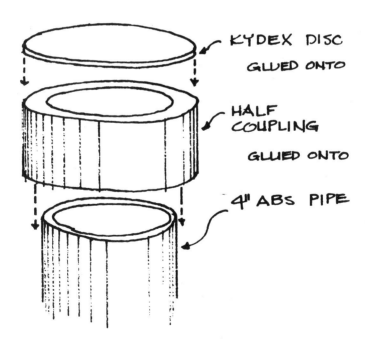

KYDEX DISC
GLUED ONTO

HALF
COUPLING

GLUED ONTO

4" ABS PIPE

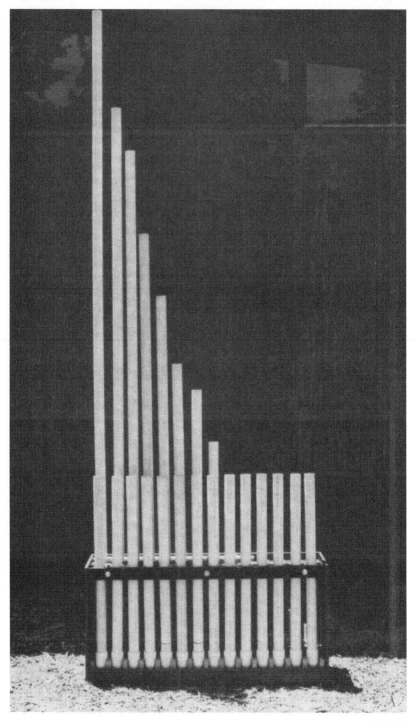

PO PIPES

PO PIPES

Polyvinyl chloride (PVC) is not thought to be the environmental demon it once was. It has some excellent uses in instrument building and it is cheap. It comes, as tubing, in a wide variety of sizes and is easy to cut, is light, and it's readily available.

We were poking around a junkyard one day when we picked up a long length of PVC pipe and hit the end of it. The result was a deep, soft, warm sound. The only problem was how to take a 10-foot piece of pipe and turn it into a playable and portable instrument. What we ended up with was the following:

The instrument was originally called a palm organ since it looks like a stand of organ pipes and is played with the palms of the hands. But somehow that name didn't sit right and so we abbreviated it to Po Pipes in honor of Li Po, the Chinese poet who celebrated wine and flowers.

A hardware or plumbing supply store will be your best source of PVC pipe. It comes in 20-foot lengths and runs around $5 to $6 per length for the thinwall 2-inch diameter we used. Wider or narrower can be used, but don't make it too wide for your palms or too narrow, as that will pinch the sound. We ended up with fourteen pipes in a diatonic scale and solved the problem of how to play it by making the pipes double back up—see drawing.

The front bank of pipes is 41 inches high. You can go higher or lower depending on your own height, whether you're partial to wearing platform shoes, etc., but you'll have to adjust the length of the rear bank of pipes accordingly.

The rear bank has a series of pipes in these sizes:

Note	Length	Note	Length
D	11'–10"	D	3'–8"
E	10'	E	3'
G	7'–7"	G	1'–11$\frac{1}{2}$"
F	9'–2"	F	2'–8$\frac{1}{2}$"
A	6'–5"	A	1'–7"
B	5'–2"	B	10$\frac{1}{2}$"
C	4'–8"	C	8"

We tuned it with a pitchpipe, but an oscilloscope or strobe tuner would be more accurate. If you cut off too much pipe, you can always lower the pitch by adding a coupling.

To allow the pipes to bend back up, you will need two elbows and a $2^{1}/_{2}$-inch length of the same diameter pipe. Glue the two elbows to the short piece to form a U-turn. Use PVC solvent cement as your glue. Then glue the front pipe sections in the elbows as shown The rear pipes we left unglued so that we could remove them when transporting the instrument. Next, round the edges of the front pipe with a file and some sandpaper. This makes the playing surface smoother and softer and easier on the hands. (Sounds like a soap commercial.)

Next comes the stand. This is the most difficult part in building this instrument. But there's no way around it, and if you can design an easier-to-build, lighter version than the one we've done, by all means go ahead and do it. And then write and tell us about it.

We constructed an open-fronted box $11^{1}/_{2}$ inches deep by 4 feet 6 inches long by 2 feet high out of $^{3}/_{4}$-inch plywood. It's very sturdy—and very heavy. You may want to try it with $^{5}/_{8}$-inch or even $^{1}/_{2}$-inch plywood. And if you decide to use more or less than the fourteen pipes in our version, you will have to adjust your overall dimensions accordingly. One of the purposes of the stand is to keep the pipes not only vertical but also to allow them to have a little give so that your hands don't absorb the full force of the blow when you play on it.

We put a 1-inch layer of foam on the bottom, protected by a 3-inch high board that runs the length of the stand. Between each pipe is a 2 by 9-inch piece of 1-inch foam and all of this is held together by a 4 foot 4-inch length of 1x3 board bolted down in three places to the bottom of the stand.

Holding the upper part of the pipes stable is the following contraption: Two 4 foot 4-inch lengths of 1x3s with $8^{1}/_{2}$-inch lengths of 1x1s in between $3^{3}/_{4}$ inches apart on center. There are three 12-inch long machine bolts in place of the 2nd, 8th, and 14th studs. These bolt into another 4 foot 4-inch length of 1x3 and attach to the back of the stand.

Handles on both ends of the stand allow some degree of portability, although anything is portable if you are big enough or there

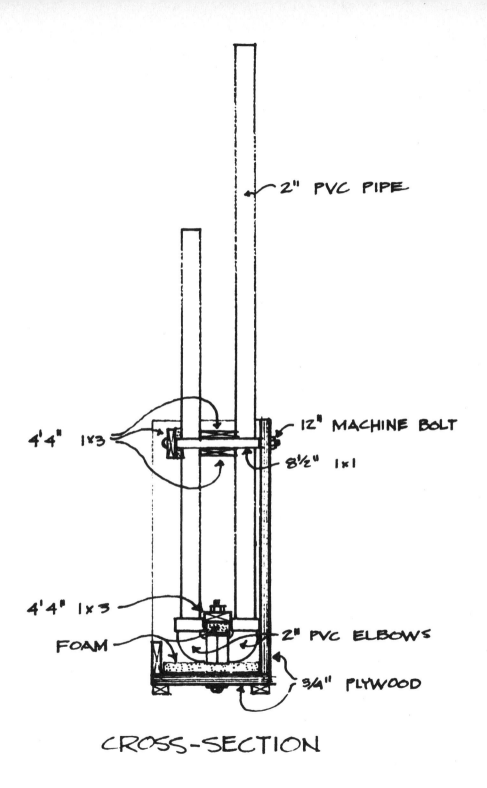

2" PVC PIPE

12" MACHINE BOLT

4'4" 1x3

8½" 1x1

4'4" 1x3

FOAM

2" PVC ELBOWS

¾" PLYWOOD

CROSS-SECTION

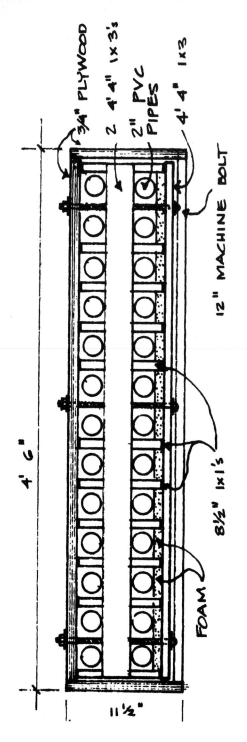

¾" PLYWOOD

2 4'4" 1×3's

2" PVC PIPES

4'4" 1×3

12" MACHINE BOLT

8½" 1×1's

FOAM

4' 6"

11½"

PLAN VIEW

are enough of you. Have you ever seen handles on the sides of the Great Pyramids of Egypt?

For added sonic interest, you might try dropping microphones down as many pipes as you have mics for. Wrap each one in a collar of foam so that it won't rattle around. Then run the mic cables into a mixer and from there into an amp and speakers. You will have an extraordinary sound that is both richly melodic and thunderously deep, guaranteed to shake loose any cobwebs in your house and perhaps in your head, too.

FUNNELODEON

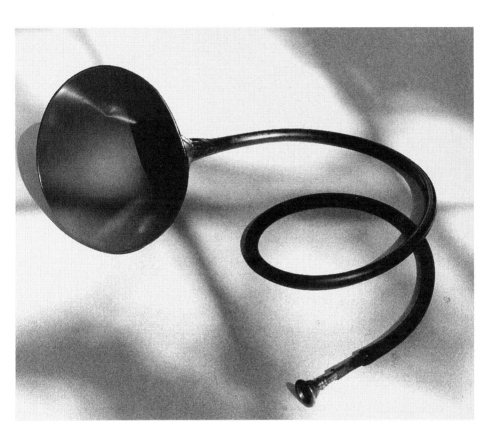

The funnelodeon came about as a by-product of Jon's classes in Music for Dance at the University of Utah. One of the assignments was to find or build an unconventional instrument. This delightful bit of acoustic craziness was brought in by Michael Arnow. For starters you will need a horn mouthpiece. One from a trombone or baritone would be best, but tuba, trumpet, or French horn mouthpieces are acceptable. These all can be found at most music stores. We've occasionally seen them at the flea market.

To the end of your mouthpiece attach a 3-inch length of $^3/_8$-inch clear plastic hose. This in turn is attached to a 6-foot length of $^1/_2$-inch hose fitted to the end of the funnel. You should use glue and electrical tape at each end of the joints since the playing technique involves a measure of reckless abandon.

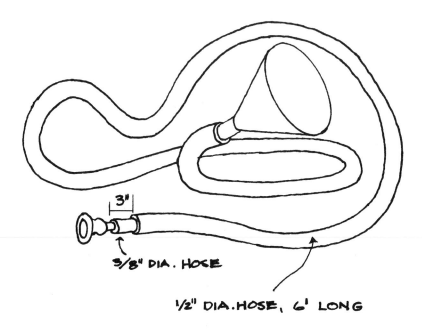

3"

3/8" DIA. HOSE

1/2" DIA. HOSE, 6' LONG

Blow into the mouthpiece, and while producing a tone whirl the funnel in the air like a sling. Increasing the speed of the funnel and changing the pitch in the mouthpiece will give you a variety of unusual sounds and effects. If a mouthpiece is unavailable, use a piece of $^3/_4$-inch hose outside your other hose. Shaving the edges to round them off will make it easier on your mouth. The trick to using any mouthpiece is that you force air past your tightened lips to make them buzz thinly yet noisily. The mouthpiece then amplifies and directs that vibration down the tube. You can even get a unique sound just by blowing in a piece of garden hose and whirling the other end.

PAN PIPES

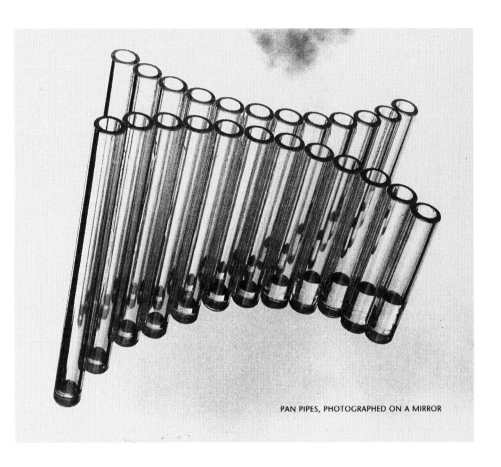

PAN PIPES, PHOTOGRAPHED ON A MIRROR

In one form or another, pan pipes are common throughout the world. In parts of South America and Eastern Europe they are played with startling virtuosity.

We first tried making a set out of $1/2$-inch thinwall electrical conduit, with corks in the bottoms for stoppers. They played OK but they were a touch heavy, and they needed lots of reaming and filing to remove the burrs left in the cutting process. So we decided to make a set of pipes out of Lucite. Here's how it's done: At a plastics supply store select a 6-foot length of 3/4-inch o.d. 1/2-inch i.d. Lucite tubing. Match this with a piece of solid Lucite 1/2 inch in diameter. It is important that you check to see that the solid piece fits inside the tubing. Each piece may vary slightly in size and the difference of a few hundredths of an inch can be the difference between too tight a fit which will crack the pipes or too loose which will give you an improper seal.

The following chart gives the dimensions of this twelve note set:

Note	Length of Pipe	Size of Plug	Total Inside Length
G	8 3/4"	1/2"	8 1/4"
A	7 3/4"	1/2"	7 1/4"
B	6 7/8"	1/2"	6 3/8"
C	6 5/8"	1/2"	6 1/8"
D	5 7/8"	1/2"	5 3/8"
E	5 1/4"	1/2"	4 3/4"
F	4 15/16"	1/2"	4 7/16"
G	4 11/16"	1/2"	3 15/16"
A	4 7/16"	1"	3 7/16"
B	4 1/16"	1"	3 1/16"
C	4 1/16"	1 1/4"	2 13/16"
D	3 3/4"	1 1/4"	2 1/2"

You can, of course, experiment with other diameters of Lucite and your measurements will be different but proportional.

Cut your lengths on a band saw, sabre saw, or hacksaw. A radial arm saw is a bit too aggressive for this brittle substance.(Whenever you cut, make sure the work piece is secured firmly.) Next, take the solid Lucite and insert it the correct distance into a pipe. Check the

pitch of the pipe against a reference note or with an electronic
tuning device. Mark the length
of the plug, remove and cut it,
coat it with solvent cement—
I.P.S. Weld-on #4 acrylic plastic
cement or its equivalent is recommended—and reinsert it into
the pipe. After you have put
stoppers in all the pipes and

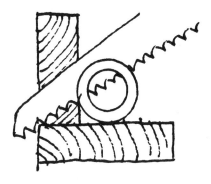

checked their pitch, bevel the blowing edge of each pipe by sanding
lightly with a sanding block.

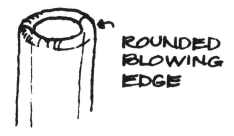

ROUNDED
BLOWING
EDGE

Now, glue the pipes together making sure the tops are all in a
straight line. Glue first with Weld-on #4, gluing one side then the
other. Allow to dry overnight. Now apply a thicker glue such as
I.P.S. Weld-on #1784. This can best be applied with an eyedropper
so that the glue falls cleanly into the grooves. Again, glue both sides
and allow to dry overnight.

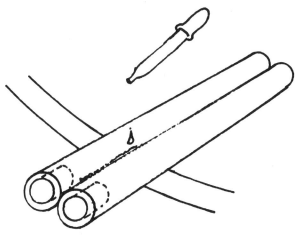

We gave our set a gentle curve in the style of the Eastern European pan pipes. We took a piece of flexible metal and clamped it together in a circle so that the arc of the circle duplicated the curvature we wished to attain with our pipes. We cut two pieces of wood to fit inside the circle and act as braces. Then we laid the pipes in one by one and glued them together. Make sure you handle the pipes with extra care during the gluing process. It is quite easy for them to come apart if they are moved about too much. However, once the glue is thoroughly dry, the instrument is quite sturdy. Note that what appears to be a double set of pipes in the photo is just one set on a cloud-filled mirror.

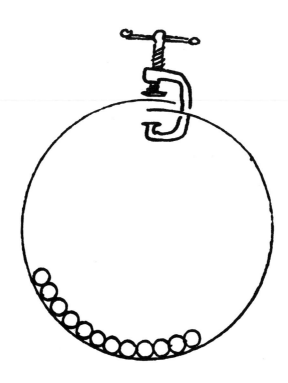

GLASS

CLOUD CHAMBER BOWLS

CLOUD CHAMBER BOWLS

One of the simplest and most beautiful of homemade instruments are Cloud Chamber Bowls. This is the name Harry Partch gave to the glass gongs that he fashioned by cutting 12-gallon pyrex chemical solution jars in half. Their tone is both rich and gentle, and when several are played together they produce a dreamlike sound.

Partch got his jars by picking up leftovers from the physics lab at U.C. Berkeley where they were doing so-called "cloud chamber" experiments. If you live in a college town you might try this. Or if you don't mind slightly inferior glass quality (though of equally good tone), try your local bottled water distributor. They usually have 5-gallon carboys that are chipped around the mouth of the jar, which they will sell to you at a fairly good price. Nice thing about these is that when cut in two, both halves can be used as gongs. However, it's difficult to obtain carboys cheaply. They usually run $10 to $20—even for chipped ones. And with the bottled water companies going to plastic, glass carboys are becoming scarce. The alternative is to forego some of that nice low tone that a carboy will produce and instead make your gongs out of gallon jugs. These can be had for free and in good condition at any recycling center. Or better yet, throw a party and there're sure to be at least four or five empty wine jugs by the next morning, along with hangovers and pleasant memories. We even made a set of sweet sounding high-pitched gongs out of the half gallon size jars.

Now the next step, and the only difficult one, is cutting them. If you have an extra ten dollars and are interested in making your own glasses, chimes, and recycled tumblers, you might invest in a Fleming Jug and Bottle Cutter or its equivalent. We have one, and it's particularly useful for cutting irregular surfaces. But there's always a way to do it without one of those fancy jigs which come with most of the commercial bottle cutters. Simply use a can and a glass cutter. Take the labels off and wash your bottles. Collect a few tin cans of varying heights, and clear off a work space on your kitchen table that is well lit. Get a candle, ice cubes, sunglasses or safety goggles, a little household oil, and your cutter. Put a thin film

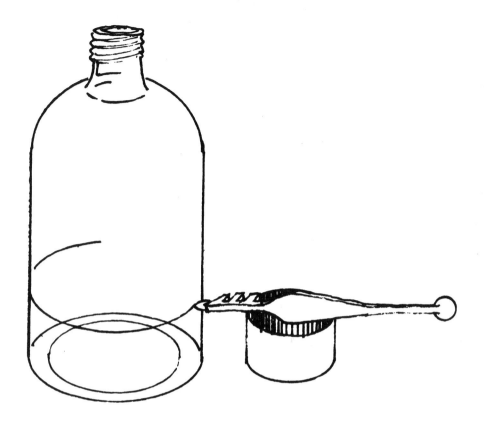

of oil or WD-40 on the cutting wheel. Take a can, say tuna fish size, and place your cutter on top, holding down firmly with one hand. With the other hand, place your bottle against the edge and pressing it just hard enough against the cutter to make a light scoring mark (this is crucial) rotate the bottle around (keeping it firmly on the table all the while) till you have scored a circle around the perimeter of the bottle once. Do not attempt to go over the mark twice. Doing that, or making the initial mark with too much pressure, may produce a jagged or zig-zag fracture mark.

Light your candle. Instead of putting it under a bushel, secure it to a jar top. Put on some leather gloves, and think about where the broken glass may go if it decides to go where you don't want it to go. Holding your bottle above the flame by both ends, rotate the scored mark, always keeping the flame 1/4-inch beneath the glass.

Hold the jar above the flame for at least ten seconds for each 1½-inch section. Then rotate the bottle slightly to the next area. After you have heated between four and five inches, put the bottle down and quickly draw an edge of the ice cube along the heated mark. You should observe the glass suddenly fracture evenly along that area. If not, repeat the heating process, this time holding the glass above the flame for slightly longer. When you have succeeded in producing a fracture, continue the process around the rest of the bottle. You may find after you have gotten your fracture mark a little way along, that merely heating it ½-inch in front of the fracture will keep the crack going and you won't have to keep returning to the ice cube. Should the fracture veer off the scored mark slightly, stop right there and restart the whole process, either going the other way or at least 90 degrees from the point where it veered. Remember, you're not trying to make perfect bowls, merely glass gongs—so slight irregularities along the edge will not necessarily interfere with the tone. When the fracture is complete around the circumference of the bottle you will be able to gently lift the top off and have a bowl and a gong, or two gongs, or if you are a gardener, a miniature greenhouse to protect your seedlings and transplants.

To hang your Cloud Chamber Bowls, tie the end of a sturdy cord to a washer. Thread the other end through a small funnel and then pull it through the mouthpiece of your bottle and attach it to a stand. Use *soft* mallets to play this instrument.

CRYSTAL MARIMBA

If you have ever heard recordings of Mozart played on a glass harmonica, or run the moistened end of your fingers around the edge
of a wine glass, then you won't be surprised at how musical glass
can be.

This instrument with its cool, gentle tone is very similar in design to the redwood marimba. The bars, however, are $1/4$ by 2-inch plate glass. You can get them from any glass dealer who will cut them and, if requested, sand the edges for you. The measurements we give are C major for a diatonic tempered scale starting with F 174.6 cps. The lengths of the bars are:

$16\,{}^3/_4{}''$	$13\,{}^5/_8{}''$	$10\,{}^1/_2{}''$
$15\,{}^7/_8{}''$	$12\,{}^{15}/_{16}{}''$	$9\,{}^{15}/_{16}{}''$
$15''$	$12\,{}^{13}/_{16}{}''$	$9\,{}^3/_4{}''$
$14\,{}^1/_{16}{}''$	$11\,{}^{13}/_{16}{}''$	$9\,{}^1/_8{}''$
	$11\,{}^1/_8{}''$	

Know that two bars of identically sized glass may have slightly different densities and thus slightly different pitches. So you are advised to purchase the bars in 4-foot lengths and cut them to the right length yourself, making whatever adjustments are necessary. Cutting glass this size is easy. Using a glass cutter and a square, score a line across the bar. Place the bar on a towel at the edge of a table, and snap down on it firmly. For cuts smaller than $1/2$-inch you should use wide-edged glass pliers designed expressly for this purpose. Or try visegrips. The rough edges can then be smoothed out by careful use of a fine-toothed file followed by sanding with a fine grit carborundum paper. As with the redwood marimba, cut and tune the longest bars first. Then, if you should happen to raise the pitch too much, you can always use that bar for a higher note.

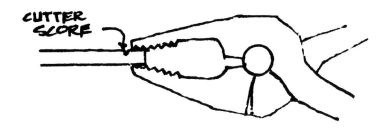

CUTTER
SCORE

After your bars are cut, find the nodes—22.5% of the distance from the end—and glue a 1½-inch long strip of ¼-inch thick neoprene or ensolite to each node. Silicon glue would be your best choice. After several months or longer of music making, various glues dry out and the glass bars detach themselves. So be alert to re-gluing periodically.

See the section on stands in the Redwood Marimba section for construction details. Glue down two 1¼ by 1¼-inch wooden rails and a strip of ensolite on each rail. Insert the resonators into the appropriate holes, and finally, using contact cement, glue the glass bars at the nodes down to the ensolite rails. This will save you the embarrassment and noise of having a bar bounce off onto the floor while you are playing.

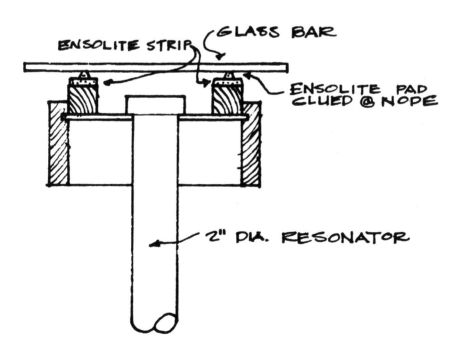

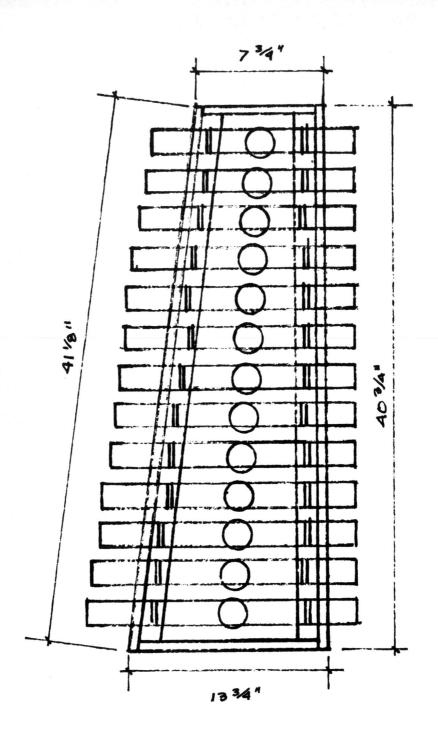

BALL JAR DRUMS & WATER DRUMS

The effect of sound passing through water is unusual. One of the ways of achieving this is by using any wide-mouthed jar with some water in it as a drum. We've found that large peanut butter jars and large-mouth Mason jars work splendidly. The bigger the jar, the more varied and louder the sound. Simply add a few inches of water, tighten the cap securely, and play with a superball mallet or your fingers while turning the jar around and about. If you use peanut butter or large mayonnaise jars, make sure the cap has a rubber gasket on the inside or you'll have waterfalls where you wanted music.

A more elaborate water drum can be made from a restaurant steam table pot. Glue several turns of heavy cord onto the pot just underneath the lip and then wrap tape over the cord to smooth it out. Now soak and stretch a drum head over the top, stapling it to the cord. A small hole drilled in the side of the pot will enable you to add water as necessary. And a cork or a piece of tape for the hole will keep the water off your lap when you play with too much enthusiasm.

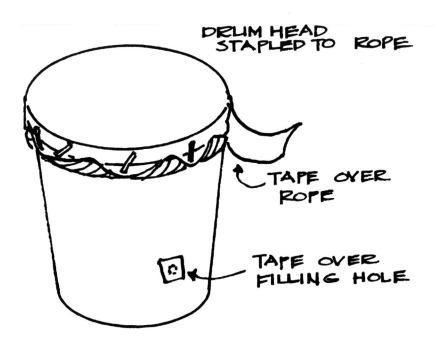

DRUM HEAD
STAPLED TO ROPE

TAPE OVER
ROPE

TAPE OVER
FILLING HOLE

FOUND SOUND

In some way, the essence of this book is contained in this short chapter. Music is where you find it. It is in the sound of a door opening, the wind blowing, children calling out at a playground, church bells, traffic, the beautiful music of language and dialects, the sound of your nervous system, and the sound of the blood moving past your eardrums (you have to listen with care for those two sounds—a quiet spot in nature is a good place to start—but they are always there.) And if music is where you find it, many musical instruments are waiting to be discovered.

Gongs and bells, in particular, can be found in many disguises at the flea market, junkyards, or in your shop or kitchen. We've gotten into the habit of hitting almost every metal object we see lying around. In doing this it is important to find the node where the metal won't vibrate and where the pressure of your fingers will not interfere with the sound. Often, a piece of oddly shaped metal will sound dissonant or lifeless until you locate the node and strike it with the appropriate mallet. Suddenly whole new tone qualities may appear.

Here is a list of gongs and bells which not only sound good but also require little if any work on your part to manufacture: Alarm bells found on abandoned factories. Filling station bells. Telephone bells from abandoned telephones found in abandoned factories. Old alarm clock bells. New alarm clock bells from alarm clocks hurled out the window. Old or new, the sound of the bells is small but sweet. Artillery shells and 20 mm or larger shell casings. Brake drums, particularly the ones from older (pre-'50s) cars or large trucks. Some aluminum bell housings for transmissions. Aluminum tubing either square or round. Gas cylinders. Hole saws available at the hardware store and costing from $2 on up, depending on their size. Circular saw blades. Most heavy metal manufacturing scraps cut round. Stainless steel pot tops and heavy-duty cake pan tops. Plow disc blades. Dust pans. Stainless steel mixing bowls. Steam table pots. Flower pots. Different sized bottles. And wine glasses played with soft mallets or moistened fingertips along the edge.

Gongs and bells aren't the only instruments that can be "found." You can fashion drums out of wooden boxes of all shapes and sizes. The Colvig-Harrison instrument array even includes bass drums made from inverted galvanized garbage cans. Wonderful sounding plastic drums can also be found, in sizes from 5 gallon buckets to large 55 gallon containers. Or try the sounding board, frame, and strings of junked pianos. They can be tuned to a diatonic scale and turned into a giant zither.

And of course there are always washboards and combs and toilet paper. Or empty beer cans tapped near the hole with your fingers. Hollow gourds, large round stoneware pots with small openings, seed pod shakers, bird calls (the Aububon style made from wood with a pewter twister are gems).

Or for an unusual sonic tweak, take two pieces of thread and attach one end of each to a lightweight stove or refrigerator rack. Hold the other ends in your ears and ask a friend to strike the rack gently with a large spoon or wooden dowel.

Bart Hopkin, who, more than anyone, has nurtured the expanding experimental musical instrument movement in this country (see Bibliography) wrote to suggest the following sources of Found Sound: Corrugated tubing to make Corrugahorns—best bet is the smaller diameter flexible hose used to connect gas lines to stoves and heaters. Get a 12"–18" piece and blow through one end. You'll hear a number of wondrously eerie pitches that are based on the overtone series.

Scrapwood xylophones. Using driftwood or any random pieces from a scrapwood pile, you will be surprised at how easy it is to assemble a nice sounding randomly-pitched xylophone by laying pieces of wood across two support pieces. It's great for beach music.

A favorite of Bart's is empty plastic caulk tubes (the kind used in caulking guns.) Hold it by the nozzle (which should be plugged and probably *is* plugged by leftover caulk) and bonk the side of the tube on your knee, or table edge, or whatever. Cut tubes to different lengths for different pitches. Cardboard caulk tubes don't work as well.

Pop bottles and jugs blown over the rim. We've all fooled with this sound. But Bart suggests that instead of tuning them by adding water, which will only evaporate or, worse, grow mold, tune them by adding sand. However, if these bottles and jugs are to be played like bells, by striking them with a stick or mallet, then you'll need to tune them with water.

Superball mallets against lots of surfaces, including window panes, sides of cars, wooden xylophones, cymbals, gongs, etc. make moans and groans and whale sounds.

Picket fences and bicycle spokes. Every kid knows about these. But in the process of growing up we often forget what we knew when we were young. Picasso once said "it took me five years to learn to paint like Rembrandt; it's taken a lifetime to learn to paint like a child."

Lots of balloon stuff: great squeaks, raspberries, Bronx cheers, etc. Put some rice grains in a balloon, blow it up, tie it shut, and you'll have nice resonant rumbly thunder sounds.

Blow down anything vaguely pipe or tube shaped. And if that doesn't work, thump on one end with your hand. Comb-and-tissue paper, two blades of grass, candy wrappers. Coil springs—large and small. Jar lid drums: one or two taps with a hammer at the center will warp them so that they pop back and forth with a satisfying sound. Bart's 8-year-old had the idea of placing them on resonating tubes cut to length for different pitches. Sand paper, coconut grater, washboard or other ridged material for scrapers. Pill bottles for shakers. In Brazil, samba musicians play little match boxes, using them both as a shaker and as a tiny box drum. In their hands it sounds like a magnificent microscopic samba band.

And lastly, Body Sounds. Music from The Original Instrument. Keith Terry, the incredible percussionist/body musician from California, has combined tap dancing, hambone, and various ethnic body styles to create Body Music. He now has a five member band to play it, *Crosspulse*. It's a very inventive delight to both the ear and eye. You should check it out.

The possibilities for found sound are almost limitless, and, since new materials are continually being developed in the metals and plastics industries, there should be an unending supply of new instruments for you to find or design. The most unlikely objects are sometimes the best, and most anything is worth a try. Just pick it up and give it a loving thump and listen. Trust what you hear.

SAMPLERS

A special note on these incredible devices. Since this book was first written, the development of sampling machines has had a large influence on popular and experimental music. These instruments digitally record and store any sound (called a sample). Once stored, they can be manipulated and played back at various pitches and speeds, and their sound envelope (how the sound appears and then fades away) can be reversed or fiddled with in other ways. They can also be overlaid with other sampled sounds, and they can be con-volved (the frequencies and overtones of two sounds are compared, and then the shared components stored as a new sound). What does this mean to you, the modest builder of percussion instruments in a small shop, or the collector of Found Sounds? It means that you can now record a few pitches of any of your instruments, and then play them on an electronic midi controller (a device which sends a digi-tal signal to your sampler or synthesizer telling it what amplitude and pitch to play—usually the controller is a keyboard or midi gui-tar or drum pad). Thus the sounds of your Temple Block or Wobble Board or Po Pipes can now be heard transposed up and down the keyboard over many octaves. These sounds can also be manipulat-ed to have new sonic characteristics, e.g., sharper attack, long decay, looped to play over and over, spliced to other sounds, or gen-erally tweaked to make whole new categories of instruments. In fact, a couple of industrious fellows even took samples of sounds of San Francisco's Golden Gate Bridge—cables and bongs and metals and creaks—and turned the results into a small symphony, played over National Public Radio. In short, a sampler is a wonderful adjunct, and will turn your musical instrument collection into a brave new sound world.

HAND MASSAGE

This may seem an odd subject to include in a book on musical instruments. But since musicians and builders depend on their hands for their craft, we thought it suitable to pass on a very satisfying massage taught to us by Shon Bong Sam, a talented musician from Korea. Also, a book authored, photographed, and illustrated by four Californians has to have at least some reference to massage, doesn't it? At least we spared you any mention of astrology.

One proceeds in this fashion: If you are giving the massage, take the recipient's right hand, palm facing up. Using your left hand, slide your little finger between their middle and index fingers, your ring and middle finger between their index finger and thumb, and wrap your index finger around their thumb. Sounds confusing? Take a good look at the illustration.

Now interlock the ring and little finger of your right hand with their ring and little finger. Still confused? Take a longer look at the illustration.

Lastly, the index and middle fingers of your left hand go around to the back of the recipient's hand where, along with the other fingertips of your hands, you push up on the underside of their hand. In this manner, the palm that is facing up stretches out and up even more. Do this firmly but carefully.
The bones in the hand, while thin, are remarkably flexible, and the hand will be quite happy to be pushed inside out in this fashion.

As you press up with your fingers, press down with your thumbs on the palm and massage it thoroughly. When all the muscles in the recipient's hand have been explored, release the fingers slowly and repeat the process on the other hand.

FOOT NOTE

The foot does not produce a particularly wide range of sounds, but it has produced an unusual array of notes. Technical papers and academic books seem to have a monopoly on footnotes. But we could hardly write a book on unusual instruments without including at least one.

And that is—if you have any questions, problems, songs, stories, suggestions, or diatribes which you wish to pass on, do write to us in care of the publisher, P.O. Box 7123, Berkeley, CA 94707.

APPENDIX

A MERCIFULLY FEW WORDS ON ACOUSTICS

One of the benefits of making instruments is that the more you build, test, and tune, the more you will understand about certain basic principles of acoustics. And it will become easier to apply these principles to your own designs, so that any new musical experiment does not have to be a totally trial and error process.

What follows is a brief description of some of the physical properties of sound—how it is created, organized, and perceived.

When one draws a bow across the strings of a Stradivarius, or blows across the mouthpiece of a bamboo flute, or clicks two rocks together underwater, or stumbles into a trash can late at night, one sets into motion a series of vibrations in the air or water or whatever medium surrounds the sounding object. These vibrations are waves that alternately expand and compress. The waves strike the skin of the eardrum of the listener, where they are converted into mechanical vibrations and transmitted into the bones of the middle ear. Here they are amplified and sent to the fluid in the cochlea, which in turn stimulates the auditory nerve, and the signal arrives at the brain. Here it's identified as coming from a violin, flute, rock, or trash can.

Our ears can perceive sounds in objects that vibrate as slowly as 20 times a second (usually referred to as cps for cycles per second—or Hz after Hertz, a German physicist). On the other end of the scale, some humans can hear sounds vibrating up to 20,000 cps. Age, over-exposure to loud industrial noises, heavy-metal rock, and other sonic curses will diminish our hearing range in the upper frequencies. Women can generally hear higher sounds than men. Only certain animals can hear beyond 20,000 cps. Dolphins, for example, can detect sounds as high as 150,000 cps.

The two main characteristics of any vibrating object are how fast it is vibrating—called frequency—and how large are the vibrations—called amplitude. Frequency determines pitch. A tone vibrating at 440 times per second produces the note A above middle C on a piano. Amplitude determines volume. The larger the vibration, the louder the sound.

With the exception of sine waves, which are pure sounds produced only by tuning forks or electronic devices, all sounds are a composite of not only the fundamental note—which we distinguish as the pitch—but also a whole series of secondary tones above the fundamental which determine the timbre—tone color—of the main note. That series is called the overtone or harmonic series. And these secondary tones are referred to as overtones, harmonics, or partials—take your choice. They are exact multiples of the fundamental. For example, the note A-440 would include harmonics pitched at 880, 1320, 1760 cps, etc.—or 440 multiplied by 2, 3, 4, on up to infinity.

We can distinguish between a clarinet and a flute both playing A-440 because each instrument has a predilection for certain overtones. On the flute, we hear the fundamental note (called the 1st harmonic) and the 2nd harmonic. All the other harmonics are practically imperceptible. The clarinet, on the other hand, emphasizes many of the odd-numbered harmonics—1st, 3rd, 5th, 7th, etc. And the trash can, stumbled into in the night, produces not only a lot of fundamental notes but a large and disorderly amount of harmonics—and perhaps a curse or two.

Here is a short glossary of music terms found in this book.

MUSIC GLOSSARY

A-440: The reference note to which all Western instruments are tuned. It is the first A above middle C on the piano and it has a frequency of 440 cps.

Amplitude: An acoustic term referring to the size of a sound wave. Amplitude is one of the primary factors in the apparent loudness of a sound and the two terms are often used interchangeably.

Bridge: A support for the strings on an instrument which also serves to transmit the vibration of the string to the sound board or body of the instrument.

Chromatic Scale: A scale divided into twelve equal steps between octaves. Not common outside of Western music.

Cps: Cycles per second. The number of times a tone vibrates in one second, which determines the pitch of that tone. Also called Hz after Heinrich Hertz, a German physicist. See frequency.

Diatonic Scale: A scale with eight notes from the first note to and including the octave. Depending on the intervals between notes, the scale will usually be considered either major or minor. For example, play any note C on the piano and then play the next seven white notes up or down and you will have a diatonic major scale. Repeat the process with the note D and you will have a diatonic minor scale.

Fipple: The plug at the mouthpiece of an end-blown flute or whistle which directs the air across an edge to produce a tone.

Frequency: The amount of times a tone vibrates in a given period of time— usually a second. The number of vibrations determines the pitch of a tone and the terms frequency and pitch are generally interchangeable.

Harmonics: The secondary tones generated by the sounding of a fundamental note. These tones are always multiples of the fundamental. Their varying strengths determine the timbre or tone color of a note. Also referred to as partials or overtones.

Interval: The distance between two notes. The consecutive notes C and D on a piano create an interval of a 2nd, C and G an interval of a 5th, and C and C^1 an interval of an octave, etc. There is a psycho-acoustic phenomenon created by intervals which makes some sound more consonant than others. Western music calls the interval of C to E^b a minor third—an interval which is "darker" or more "moody" than say a "bright" interval of a major third, C to E.

Just Intonation: A tuning practice based on the ratios of a perfect fifth (3/2) and a major third (5/4). All the notes in a scale tuned to just intonation are derived from these intervals.

Middle C: The note C closest to the middle of a piano keyboard. Western musical convention has made it a primary reference note. Other notes are generally referred to in relationship to middle C. Middle C has a frequency of 261.6 cps.

Nodes: The point on any vibrating object such as a wooden bar, a metal plate, or a wire string where there is no vibration.

Octave: A note which is eight diatonic tones higher or lower than another given note. It will vibrate at twice or half the speed of the first note. The C above middle C on a piano is an octave apart.

Oscilloscope: An electronic device which displays the frequency and amplitude of sound waves. Used for spectral analysis of sound and for tuning.

Overtones: The secondary tones generated by the sounding of a fundamental note. Term is interchangeable with harmonic except that the first harmonic in a series is always the fundamental note; the first overtone, however, is the next highest note or the second harmonic. Musical terminology, like life, is not all that consistent.

Pentatonic Scale: A scale with five different notes. E.g., the black notes on a piano.

Pitch: The quality of a note which indicates how high or low it is. This is determined by the frequency of its vibrations per second.

Scale: A series of ascending or descending notes which follow some pattern of intervals between the tones. The highest note vibrates at twice the speed of the lowest note—a ratio of 2/1 known as an octave.

Stroboscopic Tuner: An electronic tuning device utilizing a strobe light to determine the frequency of a sound wave. More accurate than a pitch pipe for tuning.

Timbre: Indicates the color or quality of an instrument's sound. Timbre is determined by the particular harmonics which are emphasized in a given note.

2/1: The frequency ratio of two pitches where one vibrates at twice the speed of the other. Commonly, but less accurately, referred to as an octave. The notes in a 2/1 interval will be totally consonant.

CHART OF FREQUENCIES

A	27.50	C	65.40	E	164.81	G	392.00
A#	29.13	C#	69.29	F	174.61	G#	415.30
B	30.86	D	73.41	F#	185.00	A	440
C	32.70	D#	77.78	G	196.00	A#	446.16
C#	34.64	E	82.40	G#	207.65	B	493.88
D	36.70	F	87.30	A	220	C	523.25
D#	38.89	F#	92.49	A#	233.08	C#	554.37
E	41.20	G	97.99	B	246.94	D	587.33
F	43.65	G#	103.83	C	261.63	D#	622.25
F#	46.24	A	110.00	C#	277.18	E	659.26
G	48.99	A#	116.54	D	293.66	F	698.46
G#	51.91	B	123.47	D#	311.13	F#	739.99
A	55.00	C	130.81	E	329.63	G	783.99
A#	58.27	C#	138.59	F	349.23	G#	830.61
B	61.73	D	146.83	F#	369.99	A	880
		D#	155.56				

WOODWORKING GLOSSARY

ABS Pipe: Black plastic tubing generally used for sewer or waste pipe. ABS stands for Acrylonitrile Butadiene Styrene.

Augur Bit: The most common bit used for boring in wood. It has a feed screw, with or without cutting spurs, and a series of spirals behind the spurs called the twist. This carries the wood out of the way to keep the drilling path clear.

Bandsaw: A power saw with a looped blade used to cut circles and odd shapes.

Bevel Square: A tool for marking or checking angles.

Beveling: Cutting an edge at an angle other than 90 degrees.

Bit: The part of a drill which actually does the cutting. See augur bit, Foerstner bit.

Bit Brace: A tool for holding bits in order to bore holes. Handbrace.

Board Foot: A standard measure of lumber, equivalent to a piece of wood 1 inch thick by 1 foot wide, 1 foot long.

Box Nails: A nail with a flat head. Used where appearances aren't important.

Butt Joint: A simple joint where the end of one piece of wood is fastened to the end of the side of another piece.

Circle Cutter: Adjustable cutter usually used in a drill press for cutting circles of various sizes.

Clear heart, quarter sawn: Refers to the best section of wood for sound transmission. Clear heart means wood without knots from the center of the tree. Vertical grain indicates that if you look at the end of the board you will see the grain running in a straight line parallel to the edge of the board. And quarter-sawn refers to a method of cutting boards so that the maximum number of boards have the growth rings close to 90° to the wide face of the board.

Cold Chisel: A chisel used for cutting metal.

Compound Lever Metal Cutters: Heavy-duty sheet metal cutters using a lever system to enable one to cut through metal more easily than with ordinary tin snips.

Conduit: Tubing used to contain electrical wire. Sometimes called E.M.T. for electrical metallic tubing.

Coping Saw: Fine-toothed saw used to cut circles and negotiate difficult turns in thin wood.

Dado Blade: A saw blade which cuts a wide groove into a piece of wood. The groove is called a dado. Also dado plane for cutting dados by hand.

Dowel: A round rod (wooden usually) normally used as a pin to join two pieces of wood. Diameters vary from $1/8$ to 1-inch. Larger diameters exist but the rod is then called round stock.

Draw Knife: A two-handled blade used to remove wood. Generally used in rough work.

Fence: A adjustable guide such as is used on a table saw or radial arm saw to keep whatever is being cut positioned properly to the blade.

Fender Washer: A large washer with a small hole in it.

Ferrule: A metal cap used at the end of a wooden handle to keep it from splitting, hold it in place, or otherwise strengthen it.

Finishing Nails: A nail with a small head. It is often used for cosmetic purposes since it can be countersunk beneath the surface of the wood. See nailset.

Floor Flange: The circular threaded pipe holder which is usually nailed, screwed, or bolted to a floor or wall and used to hold metal pipes.

Foerstner Bit: A bit without a feed screw or a twist. It centers from the outside instead of the center. It is used when you don't want to drill all the way through a hole. Or when the feed screw would otherwise interfere with your drilling process. Also used for flat-bottom holes, and can be used in carving.

Gouge: A gouge is a chisel with a concave, rounded, or U-shaped blade. It is used to dig out wood and leave rounded grooves.

Hacksaw: A saw used to cut metal. Has a strong, fine-toothed blade.

Hardwood/Softwood: Somewhat confusing terms used to distinguish between deciduous and evergreen trees. Generally hardwoods are harder than softwoods, but this is not always the case. In this book, however, when the term hard wood or soft wood is used, it is to indicate hardness or softness. The hard woods most likely to be used are maple, walnut, ash, mahogany, or fruitwoods. The soft woods to be used are redwood, pine, Douglas fir, spruce, and cedar.

Hex Machine Cap Screw: A regular bolt with hexagonal head.

I.D.: Inside dimension or inside diameter of a ring, box, piece of pipe, tubing, etc.

Jig: A device whose purpose is to hold an object firmly and accurately while some operation (cutting, drilling, etc.) is being performed on it.

Jointer: A power tool used to plane or joint wood. Also used for beveling and rabbeting.

Lathe: A machine to turn a piece of wood at high speed. By holding different types of chisels or gouges against the spinning wood, one may shape it in a variety of ways.

Level: A tool used to indicate whether a surface is precisely horizontal or vertical.

Lineal Foot: One foot long of any dimension of lumber or other material.

Mitre Box: Tool consisting of a saw and holder for cutting wood accurately at an angle.

Mitre Joint: Mitring involves cutting two pieces of wood at equal angles (usually 45 degrees plus 45 degrees equals 90 degrees), and fitting them together.

Mortising Chisel: Special one-purpose chisel, very strong, made to take hard pounding, for cutting out mortises.

Nailset: A punch used to drive nails beneath the surface—a process called countersinking. They come in various sizes.

O.D.: Outside dimension or outside diameter of a ring, box, pipe, tube, etc.

On Center (O.C.): A term used in measuring. It is the distance between the two center points of whatever is being measured. Less confusing sometimes than measuring from outside to outside, inside to inside, inside to outside, inside left to outside right, or upside down to right side out, etc.

Pipe Cutter: A device for cutting metal or plastic pipe by continuously inscribing an ever-deepening mark on the outside of the pipe. Faster than a hacksaw.

Pipe Nipple: Piece of pipe threaded on both ends, usually short.

Plow Disc Blade: Piece from a farm implement called a disc plow. The round concave disc used in tandem with many other discs to turn over the soil in a field. Referred to in agriculture as a disc blade.

Rabbet: A groove cut at the edge of a board.

Rasp: A very coarse file for shaping wood. Faster and rougher than a file.

Router: A power tool used to cut grooves and shape edges. Also can perform a variety of other functions limited only by your imagination and the bits you can buy for your router.

Sanding Block: Any device used for holding sandpaper and sanding. Can be a block of wood with paper nailed on or the commercial variety made from rubber.

Skew Chisel: A chisel with a cutting edge at an angle to the sides other than 90 degrees.

Surform Rasp: A trade name for a Stanley tool which is useful for fast rough shaping of wood.

Tee Nut: Threaded steel nut with sharp prongs, to be pounded into a hole in a piece of wood so as to bolt into it.

Threading Die: Tool used for cutting threads on metal rods—turns them into threaded bolts.

Three-pointed Files: Triangular shaped file good for cutting notches. Used for sharpening saws.

Tin Snips: Metal cutters shaped like heavy duty scissors.

Wire Nails: Thin-shanked nails with flat heads.

DECIMAL EQUIVALENTS TABLE

To find the decimal equivalent of any fraction all you have to do is divide the bottom number of the fraction into the top number.

For example: 29/32   29 ÷ 32 = .90625

DECIMALS OF AN INCH

Fraction	64ths	Decimal	Fraction	64th	Decimal
			1/2	32	.500
1/32	2	.03125	17/32	34	.53125
1/16	4	.0625	9/16	36	.5625
3/32	6	.09375	19/32	38	.59375
1/8	8	.125	5/8	40	.625
5/32	10	.15625	21/32	42	.65625
3/16	12	.1875	11/16	44	.6875
7/32	14	.21875	23/32	46	.71875
1/4	16	.250	3/4	48	.750
9/32	18	.28125	25/32	50	.78125
5/16	20	.3125	13/16	52	.8125
11/32	22	.34375	27/32	54	.84375
3/8	24	.375	7/8	56	.875
13/32	26	.40625	29/32	58	.90625
7/16	28	.4375	15/16	60	.9375
15/32	30	.46875	31/32	62	.96875

INSTRUMENTS RATED BY DEGREE OF DIFFICULTY

Just so you won't bite off more than your skills or shop can chew, here is a list of the instruments organized into groups by how much skill and/or how many tools are needed to build them. This is a fairly arbitrary grouping. Some of the "difficult" instruments are quite easy to make but their stands may be tricky. Others like the shekere are easy to make but the beadwork is time consuming. Instruments like the agogo bells and cowbells are simple but they involve welding so they have been put in the more challenging category. If you don't have many skills, and even fewer tools, start on the easier ones and work your way up.

Easy	Moderate	May Be Challenging
Amadinda	Aluminum Claves	Aeolian Harp-Zither
Ball Jar Drums	Artillery Shell Gongs	Agogo Bells
Bell Tree	Bosalabos	Balimbafon
Bull-Roarer	Chevy Cup Gongs	Carved Temple Blocks
Copper Maracas	Cloud Chamber Bowls	Cowbells
Cuica	Dimple Gongs	Crystal Marimba
Funnelodeon	Eternal Triangle	Gong Stand (welded)
Gong Stand (water pipe)	Finger Cymbals	Oil Drum Gong
Mallets, Beaters, & Bongers	Kydex Drums	Marimbula
Reco-reco	Long Gongs	Oxygen Tank Bells
Shekere	Monochord	Po Pipes
Slapstick	Organ Pipe	Red Devils
Stamping Tubes	Pan Pipes	Square Boos
Thundersheet	Rjon	Temple Blocks
Willow Whistle	Slit Drums	Tubelodious
Wood Blocks	Thumb Piano	Wood Marimba
	Tube Drums	
	Wheels of Time	

BIBLIOGRAPHY

Althouse & Turnquist. *Modern Welding*. South Holland, IL: Goodheart, Wilcox, 1992. This is the book should you get serious about welding. Complete and clear.

Audsley, George A. *The Art of Organ Building*. Dover. Good text. Covers the principles.

Backus, John. *Acoustical Foundations of Music* W. W. Norton, 1977. Thorough, somewhat technical analysis of the physics of music.

Baines, Anthony, ed. *The Oxford Companion to Musical Instruments,* Oxford University Press, 1992. We're not sure any of our instruments really need a companion, but should they look a little lonely, this would be a good choice. And particularly if the *New Grove Dictionary of Musical Instruments,* at $300 a pop, is a little pricey for you, this is the next best thing. It has encyclopedic coverage of information on a very wide range of the world's instruments.

Benade, Arthur. *Horns, Strings, and Harmony*. Dover, 1990. Introduces both acoustic principles and designs for homemade wind instruments.

Blackburn, Graham. *The Illustrated Encyclopedia of Woodworking Handtools, Instruments and Devices*. Globe Pequot, 1992. A book for tool users, collectors, or those who just want to expand their understanding of the wide range of tools available.

Diagram Group. *Musical Instruments of the World*. Paddington Press, 1976. A wondrous book. Full of illustrations and inspiration. May be out-of-print.

Doty, David. *The Just Intonation Primer*. Just Intonation Network. 535 Stevenson St., San Francisco, CA 94103. A good way to get further into intonation.

Harrison, Lou. *Lou Harrison's Music Primer*. C. F. Peters, 1971. The author has studied with Schoenberg and Henry Cowell and worked with John Cage among others. An authority on Asian music. With Bill Colvig he invents and builds many of his own instruments, and composes for them as well as for conventional orchestras. Poet and calligrapher. His book touches on aspects of his musical personality and is filled with nuggets of musical wisdom and love. Highly recommended. A new, expanded, bilingual edition of this book has been published in Japan. It is distributed in the U.S. by Frog Peak Music, Box 1052, Lebanon, NH 03766

Hart, Mickey. *Planet Drum*. HarperSanFrancisco, 1991. A cornucopia of information and history on the role drums have played in the long and, hopefully, not yet completed development of humankind.

Hoadley, F. Bruce. *Understanding Wood*. The Taunton Press, 1980. Everything you will ever need to know about wood and more.

Hopkin, Bart. *Making Simple Musical Instruments*: A Melodious Collection of *Strings, Winds, Drums & More*. Lark Books, 1995. Bart edits the unique and wonderful Experimental Musical Instruments quarterly (see below.) Because of this he has been at the center of the build-it-yourself instrument network for the last 10 years. This book is a selection of plans for making instruments, some of which are unique, but many of which have a close affiliation with standard instruments. Thus you get a design for a very harp-like harp, a very clarinet-like clarinet, a maybe-not-so-saxophone-like saxophone, tuneable drums, etc. Excellent photos, plans, drawings, and charts; everything but glue and nails. What you don't find in *Sound Designs* will probably turn up in Bart's book and vice versa. With both books in hand you could build a Philharmonic to rival New York's. Highly recommended.

Hopkin, Bart. ed. *Experimental Musical Instruments*. Box 784, Nicasio, CA 94946. The subtitle states that this quarterly is "For the design, construction, and enjoyment of unusual sound sources." It's all of that and more. An issue may deal with playing music for dolphins, ancient Greek instruments, teaching with homemade instruments, music from stones, water drums, etc. The wide range and idiosyncratic nature of the articles plus the reviews of books, journals and cassettes, make this magazine a continual delight and a must for anyone involved in building their own sound devices. Highly recommended.

Hopkin, Bart. *Principles of Musical Instruments*. Publisher yet to be determined, but will be available by 1996. This is Bart's magnum opus, a compendium of what he knows about acoustics, design, construction techniques, and sonic experimentation. Though the book is not yet officially in print, we've read it in draft form and know that it is encyclopedic. If you decide to go deeply into the world of instrument building, this is *the* book to be your bedside and shopside companion. Write Box 784, Nicasio, CA 94946 for info on availability and price.

Malm, William P. *Musical Cultures of the Pacific, the Near East, and Asia*. Englewood Cliffs: Prentice-Hall, 1977. A brief look at a vast amount of musical tradition. The book points out the main features of various ethnic musics and has a good bibliography and discography at the end of each chapter.

Marcuse, Sybil. *A Survey of Musical Instruments*. HarperCollins. A systematic look at the instruments of every culture. Suffers from a lack of photos and drawings, but otherwise it's very complete. Out-of-print, but should be available at larger libraries.

Matthieu, William. *The Listening Book*. Shambhala. This small volume should be required reading for anyone interested in sound: musicians, record producers, instrument builders, disc jockeys, audio equipment designers, sound engineers, and composers. It is both a treatise and a series of suggestions on ways to deepen one's capacity to listen. We have so much noise invading our environment that in many ways music and the sounds of the natural environment have become a debased currency. They no longer have the same power to point us towards the sacred. This book helps steer us back to having more open and innocent ears.

Mauleon, Rebeca. *Salsa Guidebook*. Sher Music Co. This is an excellent, thorough, and loving description of the history and practices of salsa, a yeasty brew of music from Africa, Spain, the Caribbean, and New York. Chockablock with musical examples and photographs. With this information you'll have a much better understanding of where your claves and marimbulas fit in the music. Available at music stores.

Moore. *Acoustics of Bar Percussion*. Permus Publications, Box 02033, Columbus, OH, 43202. Available from Lone Star Percussion, 10611 Control Place, Dallas, TX 75238. A serious look at the design elements which affect tone, tuning, and resonance of marimbas, xylophones, etc.

Newman, Frederick. *Mouth Sounds*. Workman Publishers. Incredible sounds and effects from that most amazing of all instruments: the human mouth. Includes record. Out of print but worth tracking down.

Oldham, Joe, ed. *Popular Mechanics Encyclopedia of Woodworking*. Hearst Publishers, 1994. This is a clear, thorough survey of tools and techniques, with excellent illustrations. Wear a dust mask when you read this, since you can almost smell the sawdust.

Partch, Harry. *Genesis of a Music*. New York: Da Capo Press, 1974. This is the life story and great work of the pioneer of renegade instrument builders. Complete with a long and often persuasive treatise on the curse of equal temperament. Includes Partch's theories of scales which informed all his compositions. Loving photos and descriptions of his beautiful instruments. Highly recommended.

Percussive Notes. 123 W. Main St. Box 697, Urbana, IL 61801. A quarterly put out by the Percussive Arts Society. Covering something for everybody in the world of drumming. From trap sets to marimbas to African amadina styles. The Society also has an annual convention which gathers many of the world's greatest percussionists under one roof. For information write: Percussive Arts Society, Box 25, Lawton, OK 73502.

Reck, David. *Music of the Whole Earth*. Scribners. An interesting, distinctive gallimaufry of musical theories, tastes, and traditions from many cultures. Includes pictures, diagrams, and explanations of how different peoples deal with rhythm and melody. Out-of-print.

Richards, Emil. *Emil Richards' World of Percussion*. Hundreds of photos of some of the vast instrument collection of a peripatetic Los Angeles studio musician. Distributed by Alfred Music (818) 891-5999. Recommended. Also available is Richards's *Range Finder for the Percussionist*. This is a very specialized technical guide to the pitch ranges of over 600 instruments.

Robinson, Trevor. *The Amateur Wind Instrument Maker*. University of Massachusetts Press, 1987. A thorough guide to making traditional flutes, recorders, etc.

Salaman, R. A. *A Dictionary of Woodworking Tools*. Taunton Publishers, 1986. A book for the complete tool freak, this is an encyclopedic survey of tools old and new, common and unusual.

Sawyer, David. *Vibrations*. Cambridge University Press, 1978. Has a nice selection of instruments to construct. Clearly explained and illustrated.

Schafer, R. Murray. *The Tuning of the World*. University of Pennsylvania Press. A unique book by a unique educator, composer, and instrument maker. A good complement to *The Listening Book,* it increases one's understanding of the soundscape we live in and how we are affected by the sonic environment.

Shepard, Mark. *Flutecraft*. Dist. by Monty Levenson, Box 294, Willits, CA 95490. An explanation of flute acoustics and descriptions for making a bamboo flute.

Sloane, Irving. *Classic Guitar Construction*. Bold Strummer Ltd., 1989. The standard book on the subject. Thorough.

Sloane, Irving. *Making Musical Instruments*. Bold Strummer, Ltd., 1992. Includes plans and techniques for building dulcimers, fiddles, banjos, drums, and recorders. Clear and complete.

Sorrell, Neil. *A Guide to the Gamelan*. Faber and Faber. A brief but clear overview of the rich tradition of gamelan music from Indonesia with a number of musical examples and descriptions of the instruments.

DISCOGRAPHY

Since *Sound Designs* was first published fifteen years ago, there has been an explosion of interest in the music of other cultures. Listed below are a group of recordings of music which reflect some of the instrument types in this book, with an emphasis on mallet instruments, hand drums, percussion and homemade instruments. Some are the music of traditional cultures from which we have been given many of our ideas. Others are modern explorations of new instruments. All have charm and purpose.

Afro-Cuba. Rounder CE 1088. An excellent compilation of the rich world of Afro-Cuban music. Some of the world's most rhythmically rich music comes from this small island. Here is a clear way of obtaining a visa to hear it.

Bali. Nonesuch 979204-2. The music of Bali is always beguiling and graceful. Here's a good place to start listening.

Bergamo, John. *On the Edge*. CMP 27. John is one of the most versatile and talented drummers in this corner of the galaxy. He is equally at home with tablas, frame drums, mallet instruments and the traditional trap set. Here is a good place to tap into his unique world. He also performs with the Repercussion Unit in *In Need Again*, CMP 37. This group plays everything from marimbas to roof tiles with skill and humor in great measure.

Best of Rio Carnaval. EarthBeat. One of many samba compilations which might be found in the South American section of your record store, most all of them solid representations of samba enredo, the theme songs performed during the carnaval celebration. This is centered around batucada, the extraordinarily dynamic percussion music that is the musical lifeblood of Brazil. These discs are a good place to hear what great cuica and agogo playing sounds like, along with numerous other hand percussion instruments.

The Big Bang. Ellipsis Records. A diverse and engaging compilation of the role drums play around the planet.

Drummers of Burundi. Real World 2338-2. A big influence on Peter Gabriel and many other percussionists, this is drumming from thunder's core.

Drummond, Dean. *New Band.* Mode #18 & #33. Drummond is a percussionist, instrument builder, and performer who now has the heady responsibility of being curator and caretaker for the Harry Partch instrument collection. With his group he has recorded compositions played on his own designs as well as Partch's.

Dutz, Brad. *Krin.* Interworld, CD/CS 920. Brad plays everything and the kitchen sink.

From the Pages of Experimental Musical Instruments, vols. 6-10. Each volume is one cassette containing music from instruments which appeared in the pages of the *Experimental Musical Instrument* newsletter in a given year. From soup (spoons) to nuts, the sources of the sounds are experimental, innovative, and challenging as well as lovely, abrasive, and/or humorous. $10.50 postpaid from Box 784, Nicasio, CA 94946.

George, Ron. *Music For & By Ron George.* O O Discs. Ron builds instruments. He also plays them, writes for them, and commissions others to write for his inventions. Everything on this CD is something he made, including his American Gamelan and a Loops Console.

Harrison, Lou. Music from one of our most unique polymaths. Lou is a wonderfully gifted and resourceful composer. He and his partner Bill Colvig have designed and built countless instruments. Lou is fluent in writing for them as well as for the more traditional instruments of Europe, Asia, and Latin America. For starters try *Music of Lou Harrison,* CRI 6006; *Pacifika Rondo, Two Pieces for Psaltery,* Phoenix PH 118; *La Koro Sutro,* New Albion NA 015; *Strict Songs, 1st Concerto for Flute and Percussion,* Music Masters 513616L. Have a listen, it's all there: lyricism, drama, serenity, power and elegance.

Hart, Mickey. *Planet Drum.* Ryko 206. Along with Peter Gabriel, Mickey Hart has been influential in drawing recognition to the sources of rhythm in our own music. Here is a sampling of these influences and his work outside the confines of the Grateful Dead.

Heart of the Forest. Ryko HNCD 1378. Music of the Baka of Cameroon. This is music so lovely and artless that it defies description. But do not confuse it with *Spirit of the Forest* which is samples from this music set to drum machines, an example of the worst possible way that we trivialize another culture by commercializing it.

Hussain, Zakir. Most any album, but you might start with *Zakir Hussain & The Rhythm Experience,* MOM MRCD 1007, or *Making Music,* ECM 21349-2. Son of the great North Indian drummer Ustad Alla Rakha, Zakir is arguably the most formidable rhythmatist on the planet.

Keith Terry & Crosspulse. Redwood Records, (800) 888-SONG. This eponymous first album is a unique and dynamic mix of traditional and contemporary percussion styles, plus Keith Terry's fantastic "Body Music" which is a blend of tap dance, hambone, clapping, and the kitchen sink. A must hear.

Kora & Xylophone Music of West Africa. Lyrichord LLCT 7308. The kora is a gorgeous harp instrument used by the griots to keep alive the songs and stories of their tribes. African xylophone music is, along with Mozart, a favorite way to start the day.

Ilu Anu. Fundamento 2001. Dist. by Round Records, San Francisco. Bata drumming is one of the world's most profound rhythmic approaches to tapping into the source. Deep, noble, alternately restrained and fiery, it is used to summon the sacred deities of Santeria, the Afro-Cuban religion. Regino Jimenez, the leader on the recording, is one of Cuba's greatest proponents of this style of music.

Mendes, Sergio. *Brasileiro.* Elektra 9-61315-2. Sergio Mendes? Are you thinking Las Vegas lounge act music? Think again. Sergio Mendes' album *Primal Roots* from the '70's and the more recent *Brasileiro* are two of the best Brazilian albums of the past twenty years. *Roots* (out-of-print) is the more folkloric, *Brasileiro* is an excellent compilation of recent Brazilian styles.

Los Muñequitos de Matanzas. QBADisc. Any of their albums will give you a taste of the power and emotion of the best of Cuban folklorico drum styles. Rumba heaven.

Music for the Gods, the Fahnestock Expedition. Ryko. RCD 10315. This is a release for the Library of Congress' Endangered Music Project series. It is Indonesian music at its most glorious and innocent. Only the music of the forest people in Africa is comparable in capturing this sense of wonder. Also listen to the compilations of Balinese music on Nonesuch. Glistening metallaphones, gongs, and a big sense of the eternal.

Partch, Harry. *Music of Harry Partch*, CRI K7000; *Bewitched*, CRI K70001. Music from the man who initiated much of the experimental instrument movement in this country. Wonderful, idiosyncratic instruments making wonderful, idiosyncratic music.

Reich, Steve. *Music for Eighteen Musicians.* ECM 21129. Among many of Reich's fascinating records, this album overflows with fluid polyrhythms and invention. It is also an extraordinary example of music based primarily on mallet instruments.

Richards, Emil. *Wonderful World of Percussion.* Interworld. Famed studio percussionist Emil Richards has an instrument collection which may be the largest and most diverse of any individual alive. On this compact disc of original compositions, he combines many of these instruments with his remarkable musicianship. Hear boo bams, angklungs, a flapamba, udu drums, and xylorimba among many other marvels.

Smithsonian/Folkways. Office of Folklife Programs, 955 L'Enfant Plaza, #2600, Washington, DC 20560. (202) 287-3262. What a gift to our culture. Moses Asch ran the world's most wide-ranging, idiosyncratic record company in the known universe. Southern mountain music, electronic music, readings of James Joyce's books, music of the Jivaro tribe, Big Bill Broonzy, poets and polkas, and thousands of others. Asch thought it all had merit and always kept each recording in print no matter if it sold only one copy every five years. Now our national museum has fortuitously become the curator of Folkways. They have only released some of the most popular items for general distribution. But if you write them and request a title in their catalog they will make you a high-quality cassette of the original plus a photocopy of the liner notes, all for a very reasonable price. A true service to our world's music. Catalog.

Uakti. *Mapa*. Point D164543 Marco Antonio Guimarães founded this group and built many of the instruments they use. (Some of their sounds come from instruments very like the Po Pipes design in this book.) Uakti has recorded with the great Brazilian singer, Milton Nascimento, and they are also on Paul Simon's *Rhythm of the Saints*.

Understanding Latin Rhythms. Latin Percussion Ventures, LPV110. Latin music is a heady brew of Iberia, Africa, and New York. Here is a good demonstration of how some of the music is put together.

Velez, Glen. *Hand Dance*. Music of the World 301. Also *Doctrine of Signatures*, CMP 54. The main man when it comes to frame drums.

Voices of Forgotten Worlds. Ellipsis CD 3252. This 2 CD compilation gives a survey of music of the planet's remaining indigenous cultures. As such it's a joy and a sorrow. It's a pleasure to have these musics under one roof. It is a great sadness to know that in a few generations or less, there may be no one left who knows these songs first hand.

Zimbabwe—Soul of Mbira, Nonesuch. Music of the Shona people played on the thumb piano with bright, flowing virtuosity.

TWO PLACES TO FIND THE UNIQUE, THE OBSCURE, AND EVEN THE ORDINARY IN RECORD MUSIC:

Tower Records (800) 648-4844. This big record store chain provides an equally big service by having a toll free order number. Have your credit card handy. They can get you most anything from the major distributors. But *Down Home Music* is the place to try for more obscure titles.

Down Home Music, 10341 San Pablo Ave., El Cerrito, CA (510) 525-2129, 525-7471 for catalog. May be the best specialty store around for its variety and wide selection of hard to get recorded music. World, zydeco, doowop, reggae, celtic, Cajun, r&b, if it's strange and wonderful, chances are they'll have it.

SOURCES OF INSTRUMENTS, MATERIALS, VIDEOS, SOFTWARE, AND UNUSUAL SOUNDS

Ali Akbar College of Music, 215 West End Ave., San Rafael, CA 94901. (415) 454-0581. Not only does this remarkable school offer inexpensive classes in the music of Northern India, but they also have a store which sells Indian musical instruments, cassettes and CD's. Catalog.

American Science & Surplus, 601 Linden Place, Evanston, IL 60202. Bart Hopkin gives high marks to this source which he calls "an incredible pot-pourri of useless junk, much of which turns out to be just what you didn't know you needed." Sounds like our kind of place. Catalog.

Anyone Can Whistle, a catalog of musical discovery. Box 4407, Kingston, NY 12401. 1(800)435-8863. A variety of sound makers from the quaint to the odd to cheap to chintzy. Free catalog.

Arthur Hull, 108 Coalinga Way, Santa Cruz, CA 95060. (408) 458-1946. Arthur is one of the prime movers and innovators in the Drum Circle movement in the U.S. He teaches, leads seminars, and travels around the country with missionary zeal, creating communities of drummers. He is also a partner in West Cliff Percussion, a drum manufacturing company, which sells African-style drums (see below). A video called *Arthur Hull: Guide to Endrummingment* is an excellent entry into the world of group hand drumming. It is available from Interworld Music, RD 3 Box 395A, Brattleboro, VT 05301. (802) 257-5519.

Bamboo Giant, Freedom Blvd. Aptos, CA 95003. (408) 685-1248. Bamboo, bamboo, bamboo. 8 Acres and 70 species of bamboo. They consult, sell and install this divine plant. Great for instruments, resonators, building, landscaping, and simply enjoying. They specialize in the rare and unusual hardy bamboos: Giant Moso, giant black, square bamboo, etc.

Boemia Percussion, 15510-158th Ave. NE, Woodinville, WA 98072. (206) 485-2484. Highest quality, handmade Brazilian percussion instruments: surdos, cuicas, tamborims, pandeiros, and repiniques. A bit pricey, but if you take your samba seriously then this may be the source for you.

Cosmic Aeropolane, 1305 South 900 East, Salt Lake City, UT 84105. (801) 487-9505. A shop full of color, sound, and Marley's ghost, specializing in reggae music and hand drums. They do mail order and carry an excellent line of African drums plus American-made instruments.

Denny's Sound & Light, Box 12231, Sarasota, FL 34278. They distribute a piece of software called Micro MIDI Terminal for re-turning your synthe-sizer to just intonation. IBM compatible.

Earthshaking Percussion, Box 18372, Atlanta, GA 30316. (404) 624-3349. David Strohauer specializes in Australian-style didjeridus, clay pot drums, marimbas, and cajons, as well as custom-built unique percussion instru-ments made out of ABS. Beautifully fashioned. His company also distrib-utes a line of handmade instruments from Australia, Africa, South America, the Middle East, and India. Catalog.

Eastern Star Trading Company, 624 Davis St., Evanston, IL 60201. (800) 522-0085. A good source for various sizes of bamboo for resonators, boobams, and all the other myriad musical possibilities that this glorious grass might suggest.

Elderly Instruments, 1100 N. Washington, Box 14210, Lansing, MI 48901. A big, thorough catalog of traditional folk instruments, guitars, banjos, etc. Also some more exotic items like dijeridoos. They distribute world and folk music albums and instructional videos as well. Catalogs.

Emu Systems, 1600 Green hills Road, Scotts Valley, CA 95066. (408) 438-1921. These techno-wizards design and manufacture some of the best samplers on the planet. Their prices are good and their manuals are very clear. They also believe in innovation, and thus they design features into their instruments which other manufacturers overlook. Their recently released model ESI 32 is a great value. Build some instruments and then sample them. It will allow you to enter new parallel universes. Then convolve and process the samples and it will put you on the bridge of the sonic equivalent of the starship Enterprise.

Frog Peak Music. Box 1052, Lebanon, NH 03766. tel/fax 603/448-8837. Frog Peak is an artist-run organization which publishes scores and distributes recordings of experimental and unusual works. They have been very involved in the new American gamelan movement and feature many pieces in that genre. Catalog.

Glen Velez, *The Fantastic World of Frame Drums*. Interworld (see below.) A fantastic video demonstration of the limitless possibilities of frame drums. Exercises for the beginner as well as ear food for the pro.

The Gourd Factory, Box 55311, Stockton, CA 95205. (209) 943-5852. A good source for dried gourds to make shakers, resonators, and rattles and whatever else your imagination suggests. To visit, call in advance for appointment and directions. To order, call or write for price list, or send drawing and description of needs.

Interstate Music Supply, Box 315, 13819 West National Ave., New Berlin, WI 53151. Catalog. Band instruments, music stands, Beethoven t-shirts, cork, mouthpieces, trombone slide grease, strings, metronomes, reeds, etc. The whole ball of musical wax.

Interworld Music, RD 3 Box 395A, Brattleboro, VT 05301. (802) 257-5519. Interworld is producing a series of videos on hand drumming. These, as well as the videos from DCI and Latin Percussion, are filling a great need for access to some of the true masters of the art. Along with videos by John Bergamo and Arthur Hull, they also have available sessions with Olatunji, Glen Velez, and Layne Redmond, among others.

John Bergamo, *The Art and Joy of Hand Drumming*. Interworld (see above.) A video clearly showing Bergamo's astonishing command of a variety of hand drums. It gives the viewer technical resources, exercises, and plenty of inspiration to enter into that world. Also available is *Finding Your Way with Hand Drums* which is more oriented to hand drum ensembles and circles. Available through music stores. See Discography for more from this artist.

Lark in the Morning, Box 1176, Mendocino, CA 95460. Mail order company selling folk instruments, both usual and unusual. Along with mainstream stuff, they carry charangos, pipas, hurdy gurdies, alphorns, and (watch out neighbors) racketts, plus lots of et ceteras.

Latin Percussion, 160 Belmont Ave., Garfield, NJ 07026. (800) 526-0508. These guys from New Jersey have been the leaders in developing Latin percussion instruments for more than 25 years. You can find them in any music store. Well built and reliable. Write or call for a catalog.

Lone Star Percussion. 10611 Control Place, Dallas, TX 75238. (214) 340-0835. Discount prices on drums, mallets, and percussion instruments and accessories. They also carry a line of books on the care and feeding of percussion instruments. Catalog.

Mid-East Mfg., 808 E. New Haven Ave., Melbourne, FL 32901. A source of skins for drum heads. $50 minimum order. Lower prices than United Rawhide, but lower quality control also. Good source if you have to buy large quantities.

Musicmaker's Kits. 423 South Main St., Stillwater, MN 55082. Kits for harps, harpsichords, and other unique instruments.

The Nature Sounds Society, c/o The Oakland Museum, 1000 Oak St., Oakland, CA 94607. This group is dedicated to the recording and preservation of all the sounds of nature (while there are any left). They publish a journal and organize field trips and workshops on recording sounds in the wild. An article on their activities appeared in the April 1995 issue of *Smithsonian.*

Pete Engelhart, Box 925, Loyalton, CA 96118. Pete is, among many facets of his musical personality, a sculptor who has designed an impressive array of instruments from metal. They combine aural innovation with visual beauty, and are played by thousands of musicians from Airto and Alex Acuna to the Rolling Stones. Distributed by Rhythm Tech and found in most good music stores. Pete also does custom work, so if you need say a series of bells shaped in the signs of the zodiac, drop Pete a line.

Remo, 12804 Raymer St., No. Hollywood, CA 91605. (818) 983-2600. Along with Latin Percussion, Remo has done a great service to the drum community by an innovative approach to making instruments both traditional and modern. Their African-style djembes, for example, are all made out of man-made materials with a good sound and great price. Arthur Hull has designed a signature series for Remo. Available in most music stores.

Rhythm Fusion, Box 3226, Santa Cruz, CA 95063. phone: (408) 423-2048; fax: (408) 423-2073. A very unique and wonderful store. They have as wide a range of (mostly) percussion instruments as we've ever seen under one roof. Conga drums, dumbeks, udu drums, frame drums, Turkish cumbuses, Indonesian gongs, kelp shaman rattles, zils, ganzas, surdos, and hundreds of others with equally exotic names and sounds. Plus books, CD's, and tapes. Handles mail order. Write for catalog and price list.

Sol Percussion, Box 170422, San Francisco, CA 94117. (415) 468-4700. In the first edition of *Sound Designs* we listed Valje drums as a high standard for conga drums. Unfortunately they suffered several changes, including a fire which effectively destroyed the company. Now Akbar, who helped build them during one of their incarnations, has started his own company Sol, which promises to continue the Valje tradition of high-quality handcrafted congas. He also will repair any hand drum.

Soundscape Productions, Box 8891, Stanford, CA 94309. Their Just Intonation Calculator is Macintosh-based software which will guide you down the long trail towards accurate tuning and trained ears.

Stomp. A dance, music, percussion group from Great Britain who started touring the U.S. in 1994 (hopefully for years to come). They find ways to take Found Sounds, brooms, trash cans, plastic containers, cigarette lighters, etc., and turn them into a music/dance event which bristles with wit and invention. Catch them when they next come through your town.

Tandy Leather Company. Outlets in many cities. A source of skins for drums. Pick carefully when looking at hides, and always hold your choices up to the light to see what imperfections or tiny holes might exist. Try to find skins with an even thickness around the perimeter.

Talking Drums. Jose Diaz, David Garibaldi, and Michael Spiro have created a unique and sparkling percussion ensemble. Combining Afro-Cuban and Funk styles, they have produced an instructional video which may be the best of its genre. It's clear, informative, and loaded with ideas and inspiration. Primarily for intermediate and advanced players, it shows you what can be done when you put Latin percussion instruments in an ensemble with a drum kit and mix it together with talent and taste. Video available from Warner Bros. Publications, Inc. (800) 628-1528 or at music stores. The group also tours. Contact ARTS, 977 East Stanley Blvd., #104, Livermore, CA 94550. A book and CD are in preparation.

Tony Vacca. *Melodic Percussion*. Interworld. You've built an amadinda or a marimba from this book. But how to play it? Interworld Music has produced a video introduction to playing simple diatonic mallet instruments. It is clear and nicely laid out and a good adjunct to this book. You've created your own instruments, now you can create your own music.

United Rawhide Manufacturing, Inc., 1644 N. Ada St., Chicago, IL 60622. Good supplier of skins for drum heads. Fast and friendly.

Wagstaff Music. 206 E. 6400 S., Murray, UT 84107. (801) 261-4555 Rick Senese and Sean Chase in the drum department provide good advice, good prices, and a growing selection of percussion instruments and instructional videos from around the world. Mail order.

Waters, Richard. Box 1071, Pahoa, HI 96778. Richard is the inventor of the appropriately named Waterphone, an ethereal sounding instrument combining stainless steel pot, metal rods, and water which can be bowed or struck and has been used in experiments in calling dolphins. He is also growing and selling bamboo. Write for a catalog.

West Cliff Percussion, 1803 Mission St. Box 148-B, Santa Cruz, CA 95060. (800) 900-DRUM. Arthur Hull and Rob Rasmussen have grown a terrific business manufactoring a broad selection of hand drums of mostly African design, such as ashikos, ngomas, and talking drums. User friendly, nicely made and reasonably priced, they are a great tool with which to become part of a drum circle.

Woodstock Percussion, West Hurley, NY 12491-9602. Garry Kvistad has created beautiful and tonally accurate wind chimes to hang in gardens or from porches. Most are tuned using traditional tuning systems which enhances the clarity and duration of the sound.

Woodwind & Brasswind, 19880 State Line Rd., South Bend, IN 46637. There's more in South Bend than just Notre Dame football. This is a large, well-stocked distributor carrying a wide range of traditional instruments—both winds and percussion. Good prices. Catalog.

World Percussion, Box 1963, Aptos, CA 95003 USA. 408/684-1486, 408/684-1657(fax) One of the best suppliers of Brazilian samba instruments: surdos, tamborims, repinique, agogos, etc. Now carrying small steel drums and African-made udu-style drums. Great selection, good prices.